# IDEA AND ESSENCE
## IN THE PHILOSOPHIES OF HOBBES
## AND SPINOZA

BY

ALBERT G. A. BALZ

Submitted in partial fulfilment of the requirements for
the degree of Doctor of Philosophy, in the Faculty
of Philosophy, Columbia University

New York
COLUMBIA UNIVERSITY PRESS
1918

# TABLE OF CONTENTS

# IDEA AND ESSENCE IN THE PHILOSOPHIES OF HOBBES AND SPINOZA

## INTRODUCTION

It might appear presumptuous to assert that Hobbes and Spinoza have been persistently misunderstood, were not the results of present-day investigations into the history of philosophy affording a continual justification of a mistrust of our histories of philosophies as commonly written. Some one has said that most exegesis is really eisegesis—and Hobbes and Spinoza have suffered from a habit of reading into their words meanings foreign to their thought. When a contemporary writer translates Hobbes's "phantasm" into "state of consciousness," or extols Spinoza as the first great expositor, if not the originator, of psychophysical parallelism, a belief in the frequent misinterpretation of their doctrines is sharpened. The most persistent misrepresentations of these two philosophers depend upon misreading their psychology or, more precisely, upon according to them a type of psychological doctrine which was alien to their ways of thought. We are so habituated to a psychology of psychical, mental, or conscious states, that we commit the error of endowing these thinkers with a psychology similarly based upon the conception of psychical existence. The purpose of the following essay is to show that this conception is inapplicable to Hobbes and Spinoza, to indicate the misrepresentations which result from applying it to them, and to point out the true character of their teaching.

It is a fact not without significance that psychology for a long time after the inception of the modern era remained an integral part of philosophy and that the latter differentiation of psychological from epistemological and even metaphysical questions was unknown to investigations of that earlier day. A fairly definite assignment of the psychological field and the disentanglement of the problem and methods of psychology from those of epistemology and metaphysics are relatively recent achievements. We have come to look upon psychology as a distinct science, with varying appreciation of the degree of its filiation with epistemology and other properly philosophical subjects. Such a distinction was not characteristic of early modern philosophers. What we today would call the psychological doctrines of a Descartes or Locke, as distinguishable from their epistemological and metaphysical doctrines, were for them inextricably bound up with the latter. The modern historians' separation of their epistemology from their psychology does not represent discriminations and classifications of which they were cognizant. Whatever may be the degree of interdependence of psychology and philosophy, it is not a negligible fact that such men as Locke and Descartes did not differentiate two such orders of questions, of standpoint, and of purpose. The latter-day philosopher may avail himself of psychological research in the solution of epistemological problems, just as he may have recourse to any or all the sciences. There he is utilizing the results of study in a field that he recognizes as distinct despite its degree of affiliation. Such a mode of thought is evidently inapplicable to a time when the relative independence of psychology had not been achieved.

Several interesting considerations, consequently, confront the student of historical systems. In the first place, since philosophy represents the matrix from and in which psychology developed through a long period, this latter science, even in its present relative independence, rests upon old metaphysical and epistemological notions that have persisted in more or less attenuated form throughout the transformations of psychology itself. Early modern "psychological" investigations were most often initiated under the auspices of what we to-day would regard as an irrelevant metaphysics, in hoped-for substantiation of antecedent philosophical doctrines; and such psychology naturally developed in the directions assigned to it by impelling interests which to-day would be regarded as extraneous and falsifying. Psychological doctrine was thus often shaped by metaphysical, epistemological, ethical, and even religious needs and purposes. The character of psychology, when it began to assert its independence, was determined by the character of its heredity. Inevitably it carried over, generally without deliberate recognition, a number of fundamental presuppositions and the general outlook of certain influential philosophies. Its terminology, since it was derived in the main from philosophical sources, continued to have the implications and connotations of the terms in general usage in the doctrines that represent the commencement of modern psychology. As a result, in modern psychological terminology there linger the traces of meanings which the terms properly possessed only in the setting of the historical systems wherein their signification was fixed.

The chief of these inherited doctrines in our psychology is the theory of the duality of existence. On the one hand, we find, there is a field of existence which is psychical and immaterial; on the other hand, there is a field which is physical and material. The attributes that define the two fields are related as logical contradictories. The immaterial, psychical order of existence is the truly 'psychological' realm; it is the order of mental states, of psychoses, of states of consciousness or, in more emotional language, of soul and spirit. The other order of existence comprises the bodily, the physical, the physiological, and the material. All existence is then matter and physical changes, including neuroses; and soul, spirit, or consciousness, including the series of psychoses. This doctrine of the duality of existence forms a presupposition and a point of departure for most of our psychological teaching, and the results of research are formulated in terms of the doctrine. It is generally accepted as a postulate. Or if the doctrine be expressly rejected as foreign to the science, it creeps into results surreptitiously through the well-nigh unavoidable connotations of terms which derive their import from the doctrine or from the philosophical sources wherein the doctrine itself originated.

For this reason our psychology has been in the main a science of mental states. The customary definitions of psychology as the science of mental or conscious states are the natural result of the view that existence is dual. More recent definitions of psychology, in which conduct or behavior, rather than mind or consciousness, is the defining term, apparently promise freedom from the assumptions involved in other definitions. In the end, however, the promise is seldom fulfilled, for the dualistic doctrine reappears in circuitous ways, as indicated by the resurgence of problems that the new standpoint was designed to avoid.

The facts of psychological observation and experiment and their explanatory formulae gravitate, accordingly, in one of two directions. They are either in and of a field of psychical or spiritual existence or in and of an opposed field of material existence. Concordantly, we have two sets of terms, or two sets of meanings of terms, in which the duality of existence persists in direct denotation or indirect connotation. The manner in which a single term, such as "sensation," refers on occasion to either type of existence illustrates how the double usage perpetuates the dual view.

The customary formulation of the duality is the principle, generally taken as heuristic rather than as final, of psychophysical (or psychoneural) parallelism. To a strict parallelist, the dual character of existence is ineluctable. If he wishes to be metaphysical, and treats the parallelism as fact and not as an expedient postulate, he may seek the unification of the two series of existents by reducing them to contrasted manifestations or appearances of one underlying reality. The interactionist opposes the parallelist, not primarily by denying the duality of existence, but by asserting the possibility of reciprocal influence between the two fields. Both schools really maintain the same tenet of the incommensurability of the psychical and the physical.

It will hardly be doubted that our psychology—and one might venture to add, common sense—derives its dualistic constitution from the circumstances of its history. It is rooted in a lengthy philosophical tradition.  But historical systems are many, and not all of them participate in the conceptions which became the guides of the growth of psychology.  There is consequently the danger of an erroneous expounding of historical systems through the indiscriminate transference of the tenor and significations of our own psychology to the words of our predecessors.  Because of this we are led to attribute to philosophies of widely differing purport a resemblance they do not really possess, and to the succession of doctrines a filiation of meaning that is foreign to it.

As has been asserted, Hobbes and Spinoza particularly have suffered from such misapprehensions.  The misrepresentation of their meaning rests essentially upon the introduction into their psychology of that dual view of existence which is characteristic of modern psychology. From this distortion of their psychological tenets there ensues a correlative distortion of their epistemological and metaphysical opinions. When we have equated the mental, the spiritual, the conscious, and the psychical, or have taken these terms as referring to a single spiritual principle or substance, and from this equation have derived the content for the Hobbeistic and Spinozistic phraseology, we have started our study of their systems with the assumption that the notion of existence as dual is, either obscurely or patently, a regulative force in their philosophies.

With respect to Hobbes, it may be asserted that the failure to comprehend him begins with the attempt to square his thought and terminology with the later distinction between epistemology and psychology. In one sense, Hobbes may be said to have had no "psychology" at all. What we call psychological facts were to him a part of the subject-matter of physics, and in no essential way different from the rest of that subject-matter.  The peculiar character of the problems and standpoint, implied in our minds by the notion of psychology as a distinct science, was beyond his ken.  If we should think of all "psychology" as nothing but physiology, and of physiology as a branch of physics, subservient to the latter's laws, illustrative of its principles, and happening to be concerned with the activities of a living organism, we would be near the view-point of Hobbes.  His metaphysics is in the main physics, and his "psychology" a study of certain physical facts that happen to be of peculiar importance because the knower is a sentient organism. The name "psychology," in so far as it connotes a science established on the foundations of psychophysical parallelism or whose field of investigations is wholly or even partly the psychical, is improperly applied to the teachings of Hobbes.  When the word is divested of these connotations, we are, of course, at liberty to speak of Hobbes's psychology.

Hobbes's philosophy, therefore, has no concern with mental states in so far as the phrase signifies conscious processes in a psychical realm of existence. Hobbes is no more concerned with mental or spiritual entities or states than the modern physicist. His devotion to the rising mechanical natural philosophy brought psychological facts within the sphere of a dynamics of nature, rather than relegated them to a separate realm. This statement the treatment of Hobbes will substantiate.

Spinoza, to a greater extent than Hobbes, is customarily misconstrued, and for much the same reason. Certain peculiarities of expression favor an incorrect rendering of his theory when his writings are approached, as generally happens, with the conception of a duality of existence in mind. The common approach is to pass from the dualisms of Descartes to Spinoza as to one self-appointed for the task of the unification of the dualisms. As with Hobbes, the most common failures to apprehend Spinoza's doctrine originate in the fallacy of ascribing to his thought the notion of psychical existence as one of its leading elements. The doctrine of attributes, the series of ideas in thought and of things in nature, are readily turned into psychophysical parallelism by interpreting the attribute of thought as defining spiritual existence (after analogy with the finite thinking substance of Descartes) and ideas as signifying psychical elements of existence, the series of which constitute the thought attribute. We have then a series of psychical thought existents opposed to a material and physical order of existents. The consequence is that there are two fields of existence, and their incommensurability follows from the contradictoriness of their predicates. Spinoza's dictum concerning the order and connection of ideas as the same as the order and connection of things is accordingly hailed as an explicit formulation of psychophysical parallelism.

One of the purposes of the following essay is to demonstrate the untenability of these several constructions. But at the very outset, a verbal obstacle must be circumvented. The misinterpretations of Hobbes and Spinoza, it is maintained, originate in that assumption of two separate fields or kinds of existence which comes to be implied by so many philosophical terms. From the negative side, the thesis of this essay is an insistence that the notion of spiritual substance and the conceptions derived therefrom must be eradicated from any interpretation of Hobbes and Spinoza which is to be adequate and exact. But in making this insistence it is verbally difficult to avoid translating the writer's discontent with the misconstructions just outlined into terms of a reaction by Hobbes and Spinoza themselves against the notion of dual existence and its derivatives. The danger is that in a furtive manner our philosophers will be represented as consciously recognizing a dualistic position as the antithesis of their own doctrines, against which they were in deliberate revolt, and the overthrow of which constituted a strong motive for the development of their own thought. One designing to furnish an exposition of Hobbes's and Spinoza's doctrines that will reveal the untenability of expositions that begin with dualisms of substance or existence, faces the somewhat delicate task of escaping the presentation of Hobbes and Spinoza as themselves essentially interested in combating such dualisms, and as propounding their systems in refutation of notions concerning spiritual substance and existence as dual.

The point is that a dualism of substances, or of body and soul, or of existence (Cartesian or otherwise), can not justly be exhibited as the point of departure for these two philosophies. The temper of the two systems does not own an active antagonism to these dualistic tenets as the animating agency that quickened the thought of the two men into vigorous life. The impelling influences lie otherwise, as will appear in the sequel. It may, of course, be pointed out that Hobbes does repudiate spiritual substance, and that Spinoza asserts the oneness of substance. But it is more faithful to the spirit of these thinkers to state that the one found the conception of spiritual substance to be at variance with his own position and foreign to its character, and, therefore, dismissed it as a superstition, while the other started with certain convictions of the oneness of substance and its nature, and consequently was indifferent to and generally neglectful of whatever dualistic or pluralistic beliefs came under his survey. This is historically more authentic, and as interpretation more scrupulous, than to see in the notions of spiritual substance and of the dual character of existence the great ideas against which Hobbes and Spinoza reacted, and in the rebound from which they were led to their several speculations. The picture of Hobbes as rebelling against Descartes's dualism, and of Spinoza as coming to relinquish it as untenable, which, without this precautionary warning, this essay might be regarded as presenting, may color the relations of the three with a certain attractive consecutiveness, but it would scarcely be historical. Such consecutiveness is more apparent than real and exact.

There is a different way of stating the point. It is hardly possible to avoid using the terms "physical," "material," and the like in a treatment of Hobbes and Spinoza. Such terms, however, are to most readers freighted with connotations of two contrasted orders of existence, and an effort is required to strip them of such implications. Now it is maintained that the significance and content of such terms when used by Hobbes and Spinoza, are not derived from a contrast between substances, or between body and mind, or between types of existence. The words are not loaded with such allusions, and when used in expounding the two philosophies must be deprived of them. And so the writer wishes to make clear that in using these terms there is no intention of attributing to the two thinkers any such latent meanings. To guard against this the words will generally be inclosed within quotation marks. Whatever reaction against these ideas is involved in the exposition which follows is directed against such implications as are frequently conveyed in orthodox accounts of these philosophers. The negative side of the thesis to be presented refers to what the writer conceives to be such misinterpretations.

The thesis advanced has a negative and a positive aspect. The negative side consists in a denial that either philosopher was actuated by the conception of existence as dual, or that the notion of the "psychical" or "spiritual" played an influential rôle in their speculations. Neither thinker conceived of idea or of thought as a "psychical" or "spiritual" entity, state, or process. The problems, consequently, of relating two opposed fields of existence and of demonstrating the correspondence in cognition of "immaterial" soul states or ideas to "material" changes in another sphere of existence do not arise as genuine problems in their systems.

The positive side of the thesis may be rendered as follows: First, it is maintained that Hobbes and Spinoza conceived of existence as one, and that this order of existence is, as we should say, the "physical." Existence is just existence, nature, the field of physical science, of "natural philosophy." Both men are content to take existence and nature as it is described by science. This is the metaphysical position. Secondly, with reference to psychological doctrine, it is asserted that with both investigators psychology is purely physiological in character. "Psychological" facts are to them just exactly what they turn out to be as physiological functions or processes—and they are just that and nothing more. Their psychology is a doctrine of the operation of the animal spirits, or in more recent phraseology, of processes in the nervous system. For Hobbes, what we should call "mental states" are physical effects; and Spinoza's opinions are essentially in agreement with those of Hobbes. Their respective psychologies are to them parts of physics; for them the distinctions between physics, physiology, and "psychology" are matters of expedience, implying no ultimate and irreducible diversity in the nature of the phenomena to be investigated.

The last element of the thesis concerns the epistemological teachings connected with such metaphysical and psychological views. With respect to Hobbes, the brain state is related to extra-organic object as effect to cause. This relation affords us knowledge of probability, unscientific or conjectural knowledge. Scientific or genuine knowledge depends upon the signification and use of the terms of discourse.

With regard to Spinoza, it is maintained that by "idea" in the epistemological sense he means logical essence. In so far as there is a "psychological" account of the idea and of thinking, ideas and thinking are explained in physiological terms as truly as the phantasm in Hobbes's teaching. With reference to knowledge the term "idea" signifies a logical entity, the pure concept. It is a truth. Spinoza's classification of ideas is logical, not psychological. All "things," happenings, events, are "physical." The correspondence of the order and connection of ideas with the order and connection of things is, therefore, a harmony of ideas or the logical truths of things as deductively ordered and systematized about and under the concept of substance, with the system of events that makes up all existence or nature. In short, his basic principle is that the coherent logical system of concepts corresponds to the orderly system of nature.

# PART I

## HOBBES

The general revolt against scholasticism assumed too many forms to enable one to summarize it in a phrase. In some quarter or other reactions against every element of the doctrine of the school occurred. The movement towards the inductive and experimental investigation of nature, of which Francis Bacon was the protagonist, was by no means limited to him. Moreover, this movement can not be taken as signalizing the whole meaning of the revolt. The rebellion had its religious, moral, metaphysical, artistic, and political, as well as "scientific," moments. Only as a very general transformation of viewpoint, of desire, purpose, and insight, can the new currents of thought be called one.

Thomas Hobbes affords an interesting example of participation in a common dissatisfaction and repudiation of the scholastic standpoint with striking divergences from the philosophical endeavors of other prophets of the new era. Hobbes's intimacy with Bacon suggests the picture of a relation of master and follower between them, but such a picture is assuredly misleading. Toennies [1] and Robertson [2] both object to such a depiction of the relationship of the two men. The true intellectual progenitor of Hobbes is Galileo. Galileo had destroyed the medieval concept of purpose as a category applicable to nature. The conception of nature as a system of mechanical forces measurable in terms of mathematics took captive the imagination of Hobbes, and was at least instrumental in the clarification of his thought, if it did not determine its course. Toennies [3] declares that the epistemological question of the time was whether knowledge attaining the level of the certainty of mathematics, of geometrical demonstration from axioms and definitions, was possible, and how it was possible. When Hobbes, relatively late in life, made the acquaintance of Euclid, it was this problem that was formulated in his mind. It was the natural consequence of Galileo's work. Galileo regarded mathematics as the indispensable prelude to philosophical study [4] and Hobbes shared the opinion. The former, according to Toennies, really inaugurated the age of mathematical deduction. Such deduction was to become

---

[1] "Anmerkungen über die Philosophie des Hobbes," *Vierteljahrsschrift für wissenschaftliche Philosophie*, Vol. 3, 1879, pp. 459–460.
[2] "Hobbes," Blackwood's Philosophical Classics.
[3] *ibid*, p. 461.
[4] *cf.* Toennies, *ibid*, p. 456.

Hobbes's ideal of method. Bacon can hardly be said to have grasped this epistemological problem; and the correlative ideal of method was not a part of his thought. In the light of this, therefore, Bacon can not be regarded as the immediate forerunner of Hobbes. Seth remarks that Hobbes's quarrel with scholasticism "concerns the subject-matter, not the method, of that philosophy. He does not join in Bacon's protest against the scholastic habit of anticipating nature, of deducing facts from theories; he has no thought of substituting a scientific induction for the deductive rationalism of scholastic philosophy. So far as the question of method is concerned, he is the opponent rather of Bacon than of the schoolmen; for him science, as such, is rationalistic or deductive, not empirical and inductive. Rational insight, not empirical knowledge, is his scientific ideal." [5]

It was, then, the teleological character of the old physics that was a chief point of reaction for Hobbes. The mechanistic character of the new physics implied a difference in procedure. In place of the older process of the classification of qualities, the study of nature in terms of quantity was inaugurated. This change in the character of physics literally meant the application of mathematics to nature. So that the new epistemological problem, the new conception of nature, and the geometric ideal of method are elements of one movement.[6]

A detailed account of the sources and of the arising and maturing of Hobbes's thought is out of place here. His attitude toward the doctrine of the plurality of substances and the cognitive correspondence of idea and object are our first concern.

When nature is conceived as a vast mechanical system, nature is but one substance. But, unlike Descartes, Hobbes does not rule the "mind" out of nature and devise a second substance in which the mental life may be conceived as taking place. Human nature is a part of nature; it is a product of the same forces; it is regulated by the same laws as nature itself. The reduction of qualities to quantities applies in the sphere of the psychological since that is but an integral part of the whole physical system. Hobbes speaks, to be sure, of the "two principal parts of man," body and mind. But no duality of substance is intended. Mind is defined only by an enumeration of "mental" faculties. There is but one substance, body. "The word body, in the most general acceptation, signifieth that which filleth, or occupieth some certain room, or imagined place; and dependeth not on imagination, but is a real part of the universe. For the universe, being the aggregate of bodies, there is no real part thereof that is not also body."[7] Spirit, according to Hobbes, originally meant air, or breath, and comes to mean

---

[5] *English Philosophers and Schools of Philosophy*, p. 58.

[6] *cf.* Toennies, *ibid.*

[7] *Works of Hobbes*, Molesworth edition, 1839, Vol. 3, *Leviathan*, pt. 3, ch. 34; all references are to this edition.

incorporeality from having originally indicated subtle body. "Matter is the same with body; but never without respect to a body which is made thereof. Form is the aggregate of all accidents together . . . spirit is this fluid, transparent, invisible body."[8] The notion of an incorporeal substance is a contradiction in terms, a vain idea induced by apparitions, hallucinations, and dreams. It is a sort of mental hobgoblin. Hobbes uses the terms "ghost" and "incorporeal substance" in juxtaposition, and is serious in so doing.[9] From Hobbes's objections to Descartes it appears that he was either unable to understand Descartes's notion of the immateriality of thought or, what is more probable, perversely refused to comprehend it. In this Gassendi resembled Hobbes. The notion of immateriality, at least in the sense of the immateriality or ideality of form, was a commonplace to those imbued with the scholasticism of the traditional education of that age. Descartes's soul substance represents not so much an innovation and a novel distinction, as a renovation of a time-honored conception, coupled with a more explicit comprehension of the implications of the reduction of a plurality of substances to two. To Hobbes and Gassendi, archheretics of the age, Descartes appeared the victim of a great superstition, as bad as that of belief in occult powers. On the one hand, in their eyes, he was proclaiming allegiance to the new science of nature; on the other, he was asserting the validity of a nonsensical notion that was one of the rankest growths of scholasticism.

The animus of Hobbes's strictures on the notion of incorporeal substance was derived not so much from a devotion to a monism of substance as from a conviction of the worthlessness of the concept of substance as such. He does, of course, speak of body substance, but concerning this single substance he really has little to say. At bottom, he is of the opinion that any and every notion of substance is vain, empty, and unfruitful. Its serviceableness, in so far as it has any, is in its use as a limiting idea. The phenomena of nature, and these include the phenomena of human nature, are motions. The science of nature is essentially the science of dynamics or mechanics—a mathematical quantitative investigation of the sequence of physical events. The new conception of nature serves, for Hobbes, all the purposes formerly served by the concept of substance. The thought of nature as a dynamical system is so fundamental with Hobbes that he seems well-nigh to confound pure mathematics with its applied forms. The true relationship between mathematics and physical science is obscured in his thinking through the discovery that nature possesses a sort of mathematical structure. And it is this vision that fructifies his thought, rather than the notion of the oneness of substance. As has been indicated, he desired to

[8] *Answer to Bishop Bramhall*, Vol. 4, p. 309.
[9] *De Corpore*, Vol. 1, pt. 4, ch. 25, p. 399.

give knowledge of nature the certainty of geometry. The practical identification of geometry and mechanics raises the laws of motion to the rank of geometrical axioms and definitions, and mechanics, as the science of all nature, thereby attains, in his mind, a position comparable to the deductive, demonstrative certainty of geometry.[10] Motion thus becomes the chief category of his thought while the concept of substance lapses from mind. For once science as the study of motion is launched, the notion of body retreats from sight; and one could properly say that the notion of substance takes the form of the conception of nature as a uniform, mechanical system. This opinion is corroborated by the fact that Hobbes seems at little pains to determine the nature of substance. Having served its purpose as a counter blast to pluralisms and dualisms of substances, it becomes a shadowy sort of metaphysical background for science. Owing to this fact, Hobbes's philosophy is sometimes called phenomenalistic. Space and time are phantasms. Accidents do not "inhere" in bodies, but are our ways of conceiving body. All accidents can be thought away from body, save magnitude. The accidents of body are phenomena of motion, and science is knowledge of these accidents. Thus natural philosophy deals with a world of motions and accidents, the relation of which to substance remains unsettled; and it so remains, probably, because Hobbes thought of the problem of this relation as vain and fruitless. Had he not regarded the notion of substance as empty, he must have raised questions concerning the relation of motion to substance. But in the main, questions of that type are left to one side.

It is noteworthy that Hobbes's psychology is developed largely in the interest of physics. Of the psychology of sensation and perception, at least, this is true. As all psychological process is really motion, psychology is a branch of physics. A brief survey of his psychology will indicate this.

The subject of sense is the sentient itself. And it is of prime importance to observe that this "subject of sense" is neither consciousness, nor soul, nor mind, but, in Hobbes's own phrase, "some living creature." Sense is motion in the sentient. All qualities "called sensible, are in the object, that causeth them, but so many several motions of the matter, by which it presseth our organs diversely."[11] These motions are propagated on into the organism. But this motion meets an "outward" motion, and this clash of motions is sense. "Sense is a phantasm made by the reaction and endeavor outwards in the organ of sense caused by an endeavor inwards from the object, remaining for some time more or less."[12] "Neither in us that are pressed, are they (qualities) anything

10 cf. Toennies, ibid, Vol. 4, 1880, p. 69; Philosophical Elements, sect. 2 ; De Homine, ch. 10, 5.
11 Vol. 3, ch. 1, p. 2.
12 Concerning Body, Vol. 1, pt. 4, ch. 25, p. 301.

else, but divers motions; for motion produceth nothing but motion."[13] In Chapter 25 of the *Concerning Body*, we learn that qualities are not accidents of the object, for light and color, for example, are merely phantasms of the sentient.

How thoroughly the psychology of sensation and perception is regarded by Hobbes as an integral part of physics is indicated by the fact that Hobbes raises the question whether there is not sensation in all bodies.[14] For reaction, as well as action, characterizes all bodies, and sensation is a phenomenon of a type describable in such categories. He falls back on the fact that the human body retains the prior motion as a dampened but persistent organic reverberation; and in this resides the possibility of memory. Or, to speak more accurately, memory, in Hobbes's sense of the term, is an essential part of sense. He does not seem, however, to offer an explanation of how the motions from sense persisting in subliminal form come to attain, when we remember, a state of excitement approximating that of the original experience. "For by sense, we commonly understand the judgment we make of objects by their phantasms; namely, by comparing and distinguishing those phantasms; which we could never do, if that motion in the organ, by which the phantasm is made, did not remain there for some time, and make the same phantasm return. Wherefore sense . . . hath necessarily some memory adhering to it."[15] Hence the "nature of sense can not be placed in reaction only,"[16] but an organic continuance of the motion, or reverberation, must be added to the action-reaction scheme. Yet it is to be noted that this does not remove sense psychology from physics, for the persistent motion is just motion in a given body. Rather it means that the physics of sense deals with an added factor.

Since all ideas are originally from sense, they are also motions in the sentient. Hobbes is loose in his use of terms, and he maintains with consistency no distinctions between images, representations, ideas, and conceptions. They are all really images. All psychological facts are motions or clashes of motions. Sense processes differ from ideas and images only in that the latter are revived motions or motions continuing in the absence of the object. All mental processes are at bottom of two kinds, either sensations (perceptions) or images. The general name for both kinds is "phantasm." "The imagery and representations of the qualities of the thing without, is that we call our conception, imagination, ideas, notice, or knowledge of them; and the faculty or power by which we are capable of such knowledge, is that I here call cognitive power, or conceptive, the power of knowing or conceiving."[17] Imagina-

---

[13] Vol. 3, ch. 1, p. 2.
[14] *Concerning Body*, Vol. 1, p. 393.
[15] *ibid.*
[16] *ibid.*
[17] *Human Nature*, Vol. 4, ch. 1.

tion is defined as "conception remaining, and little by little decaying from and after the act of sense."[18] The representative image is a state of sense overpowered by another and later sense experience. Productive imagination is the composition of motions in the brain.

The phantasm is called the "act of sense." "From this reaction by the motions in the sentient phantasm or idea hath its being." Hobbes says with reference to phantasm as the act of sense, that "the *being a doing* is the same as the *being done*;"[19] he adds that "a phantasm being made, perception is made together with it." This seems to mean that the motion process, or the clash of motions, *is* itself the idea or perception, the phantasm.

Hobbes distinguishes, or seems to distinguish, between the cognitive or conceptive faculty and the imaginative or motive faculty. "For the understanding of what I mean by the power cognitive, we must remember and acknowledge that there be in our minds continually certain *images* or conceptions of the things without us, . . . the *absence* or *destruction* of things once imagined doth not cause the *absence* or *destruction* of the *imagination* itself. This *imagery* and *representations* of the qualities of the thing without, is that we call our *conception*, *imagination*, *ideas*, *notice*, or *knowledge* of them; and the *faculty* or power by which we are capable of such knowledge, is that I here call *cognitive power*, or *conceptive*, the power of knowing or conceiving."[20] But then Hobbes proceeds to equate obscure conception and phantasy or imagination,[21] so that the distinction between the two faculties is left inexact. Certainly no distinction between image and conception appears from these citations. But while Hobbes, as a matter of terminology, does not distinguish between image and conception as existences, he has a certain distinction in use and meaning that can be most easily denoted by these terms. To make this clear, it will be necessary to turn briefly to his idea of knowledge.

Hobbes has in mind a knowledge system comparable to geometry in method and certainty. This universal system, which represents the ideal of knowledge, is contrasted with the particularity of sense experience. The opposition between the universal principle in which alone consists true knowledge and the empirical manifold does not lead in the case of Hobbes to an attempt to derive knowledge from sense experience. His problem is not stated in the form: How can we obtain from sense experience the organized body of universal principles? The contrast between principle and particular sense experiences develops rather into an antithesis that runs through his theory of knowledge. The experiences of sense are, in conformity with Hobbes's mechanistic view

---

[18] *ibid*, ch. 3, 1.
[19] Vol. 1, pt. 4, 25, p. 392.
[20] *Human Nature*, Vol. 4, pp. 2–3.
[21] *cf. ibid*, p. 9.

of nature, effects. They are not differentiated from other effects in nature because they involve a unique principle. The fact that sense effects happen to concern a sentient being does not signify that they are of an order essentially different from other sorts of effects, for the sentient being is an integral part of the mechanical system. Now true knowledge is knowledge of causes, and causes in Hobbes's system of knowledge are to correspond to the first principles of mathematics. Therefore the problem of the relation of universal principles and sense experience is formulated in terms of cause and effect. In consequence, there arises an antithesis between knowledge from causes to effects and knowledge from effects to causes.

Geometry, the model that Hobbes seeks to follow, begins with axioms and definitions and proceeds deductively to the exposition of consequences. But why is geometry demonstrable? Because the power to construct the object of thought is in the demonstrator.[22] But with respect to knowledge of fact, sense experience can not give us general notions, universal principles, definitions, and axioms. We do not know the construction of things. Science, imitating geometry, proceeds deductively from causes, which are the axioms and first principles of science, to effects. Sense experience is an effect, and, therefore, can not in any direct fashion supply the starting-points for scientific knowledge. From sense effects, or from effects generally, we can demonstrate, not the real causes, but only possible causes, of the effects. So the antithesis takes the following form: on the one hand is scientific knowledge—the only real knowledge—proceeding from causes to effects and revealing necessities of connection; on the other hand, we have knowledge of possible causes of real effects, and this is mere knowledge of probability, knowledge of experience, unscientific knowledge.

Hobbes does not give a satisfactory account of how we are to obtain the first notions of science. If, however, he does not solve this difficulty, two things aid him in glossing it over and, perhaps, convincing him that he has solved it. First of all, there is that identification of mathematics and mechanics already referred to. By analytic procedure the primitive notions (axioms and definitions of physical science) are to be secured, and then, proceeding synthetically, the effects are to be demonstrated from their causes or first principles. The body of definitions, or primitive truths, thus obtained by analysis would form First Philosophy.

The second recourse afforded Hobbes is language, an instrument that makes possible the transcendence of the limitations of experience. Reasoning is computation, addition and subtraction; and judgment is the uniting of two names by the copula "is." The universal name is a

---

[22] cf. *Six Lessons to the Professor of Mathematics*, Vol. 7, p. 134; cf. Toennies, *op. cit.*, Vol. 4.

counter or symbol, and truth is consistency in the use of terms.  The universal name does not represent any particular existing object, nor any particular image.  It may indicate indifferently any individual object of a class, or an image of any individual object of a class.  In short, it is a matter of no importance what image is attached to the name.  The essential thing is that the signification of the name be clearly determined upon and that it be accepted.

Now to return to the distinction of image and conception.  The image, particularly in so far as Hobbes uses conception as terminologically equivalent to image, is itself an existence, a motion in the sentient, a physical *effect*.  Experience is "store of phantasms," and phantasms are, as existents, effects, the source of problems.  The image is literally like the images in a mirror.  The shilling, observed through a glass of a certain figure, is seen as twenty shillings.  The shilling is a body—the images given by the glass are, in Hobbes's own terms, fancies, idols, mere nothings, echoes.[23]  The proposition that "there is nothing *without us* (really) which we call an *image* or colour" is proved pointing out that "the image of anything by *reflection* in a *glass* of *water* or the like, is *not* anything *in* or *behind* the glass, or *in* or *under* the water."[24]

Conceptions, in so far as they are composed of images, are like all other images.  But conception as a name standing for a class of objects (or class of images) and accompanied by an image of a particular object of the class, means the *term of discourse*.  What we should ordinarily intend by "conception" or "general idea" signifies for Hobbes symbolic word counters with meanings determined and agreed upon, which form the terms in the process of reasoning.  Image and conception as psychological existents are one and the same.  But with reference to knowledge, conception is the universal name standing for a group of particular empirical facts (images or sense perceptions), and knowledge based upon such terms is universal, scientific knowledge; while knowledge based upon particular images, or trains of images, is unscientific and not of universal validity.  This is clarified by a reference to Hobbes's *Objections to Descartes*.  The latter has said that he does not understand by the imagination what the wax is, but conceives it by the mind alone.  A distinction between image as physiological process and idea as an immaterial spiritual entity is thus implied.  Hobbes objects to this as follows: "There is a great difference between imagining, *i.e.*, having some idea, and conceiving with the mind, *i.e.*, inferring, as the result of a train of reasoning, that something is, or exists. . . But what shall we now say, if reasoning chance to be nothing more than the uniting and stringing together of names or

[23] *Decameron Physiologicum*, Vol. 7, pp. 78–79.
[24] *Human Nature*, Vol. 4, pp. 4–5.

designations by the word *is?* It will be a consequence of this that reason gives us no conclusion about the nature of things, but only about the terms that designate them, whether, indeed, or not there is a convention (arbitrarily made about their meanings) according to which we join these names together. If this be so, as is possible, reasoning will depend on names, names on the imagination, and imagination . . . on the motion of the corporeal organs. Thus mind will be nothing but the motions in certain parts of an organic body."[25] "It is evident that essence in so far as it is distinguished from existence is nothing else than a union of names by means of the verb *is.*"[26]

In short, in terms of psychology, there is no distinction between conception and image. Words, one would suppose, are also images. But with reference to knowledge, conception as universal names signifying a class of objects or an abstract principle is in sharpest contrast to the particular image. While for Descartes the image is what Hobbes would have it be, namely, motion (or some purely physical change) in the sentient organism, the idea or conception is an entity in an immaterial soul substance.

Mention has been made of what has been called Hobbes's "phenomenalism." In connection with the meaning of this term as applied to Hobbes certain questions concerning qualities arise. First of all, what is the "object" of perception? It is not any sense quality, or a combination of them, and merely that. The object of sight, he says, is neither light nor color (which are phantasms in the sentient), but the object that is light or colored.[27] "The whole appearance of figure, and light and color is by the Greeks commonly called *eidos* . . . and by the Latins, *species* or *imago;* all which names signify no more but appearances."[28] Now subtracting from the "object" these secondary qualities, what remains? Motion, and in some obscure sense, body, substance. Consider briefly in connection with this certain aspects of Hobbes's account of qualities.

The causes of sensible qualities, he says, can not be known until we know the causes of sense.[29] Sensible qualities from the side of the object are "so many several motions, pressing our organs diversely";[30] from the side of the perceiving subject, they are again "nothing but divers motions."[31] Qualities are apparitions of the motions produced by the object on the brain; but the apparitions or images are also said to be "nothing *really*, but *motion* in some internal substance of the

[25] *Philosophical Works of Descartes,* Ross and Haldane, Vol. 2, p. 65.
[26] *ibid*, p. 77.
[27] Vol. 1, p. 404.
[28] *ibid*, pp. 404–405.
[29] Vol. 1, p. 72.
[30] Vol. 3, p. 2.
[31] *ibid.*

head." [32]   Four propositions are advanced [33] that should be considered here: "That the subject wherein colour and image are inherent, is *not* the *object* or thing seen.   That there is nothing *without us* (really) which we call an *image* or colour.   That the said image or colour is but an *apparition* unto us of the *motion*, agitation, or alteration, which the *object* worketh in the *brain*, or spirits .   .   . that as in *vision*, so also in conceptions that arise from the *other senses* the subject of their *inherence* is not the *object*, but the *sentient*."

It would appear, therefore, that the "object" reduces to motions of body.  Secondary qualities at least depend on the organism and are *in* the organism.  Hobbes's position is, then, in general, that of modern physics.  For the physicist the given color is just so many vibrations per second in the medium, that is, a certain kind of motion.  For Hobbes as physicist, the subject-matter of investigation is the various kinds of motion.  Body is distinguished from its "appearances."  Body as a principle beyond appearances affords a problem for metaphysics rather than for physics.  Appearances as phenomena of motion form the subject-matter of physics.  Body as substance ranks as a sort of general postulate of physical science.  This seems to be, in a general way, the drift of Hobbes's meaning.

To return for a moment to the psychology of perception.  It is to be noted that while the cause of perception is the motion which is propagated through the medium into the organ of sense and then on into the brain, this motion is not in and by itself the sensation quality or the perception.  The perception (sensation) arises only when the inward motion clashes with the outward motion or "endeavor."  The "apparition" or phantasm is then not the incoming motion itself.  But then we may ask: Is the phantasm the *clash* of the motions?  Is the psychological process just this reaction upon another motion, a sort of compound motion resulting from the combination of the inward and outward motions, or is it the way in which the total motion process appears to the percipient?  There seem to be two possible interpretations of Hobbes's thought: either the clash of the "endeavour inwards" and the "endeavour outwards" *is in itself* the apparition or quality;  or the qualities *depend on, but are something more than*, the motion reaction in a nervous substance on the inward-going motion which is a continuation of the motion originating in some extra-organic source.  The "clash" is either the *apparition or sense quality itself*, or *that which appears in sense perception as the quality*.

Hobbes's own statements afford no ground for doubting that for him the clash of motions is itself the quality, apparition, or phantasm.  Or in terms characteristic of his age, they are simply movements of the

[32] *Human Nature*, Vol. 4, ch. 7, p. 1;  *cf.* ch. 8, 1, and ch. 10, 1.
[33] *Human Nature*, Vol. 4, p. 4.

animal spirits, vibrations in the nerves; the only qualification is that they are compound movements or vibrations. The idea may be untenable, the theory superficial and neglectful of real difficulties, but it is Hobbes's answer.

We may ourselves introduce the question of consciousness, in order thereby to indicate the unsatisfactory character of this psychology. But then we are injecting into the exposition of his thought an order of questions of which he was not cognizant or, being aware of them, simply neglected. Having denied the existence of incorporeal substance, he could not and would not regard the apparition or conception or image as a soul state, a spiritual event, in an immaterial soul, and corresponding to, rather than being, a physical motion. It is the result of an inadequate historical perspective to raise the question of the relation of the "clash" of motions to "consciousness," or to make the immediate object of sense a "state of consciousness" in the ordinary sense of the term (see below).

The source of misunderstanding is the question of what is meant by the "object," and to this we must return. What the object is does not hinge upon any question of a relation to consciousness, but upon the relation of the question of psychology to the question of physics. In terms of Hobbes's physics, which we must remember is essentially mechanics, the "object" is a set of "divers motions," connected in a manner not wholly explained with substantial body. The accidents of body, for Hobbes the physicist, are those divers motions. All accidents can be generated or destroyed, save those of magnitude and extension; body can never be generated or destroyed. Bodies are things and are not generated, accidents (save magnitude and extension) are generated and are not things. These statements define the subject-matter of physical science.

But the "object" as that which the sentient has, or as the content of the sentient's experience, is not precisely the same as the "object" existing outside the sentient. It is not these "divers motions" constituting the extra-organic object, but the immediate object of sense, and this is a phantasm, apparition, or combination of phantasms. Now the *explanation* of the psychological process and fact is cast in terms of physics. The external cause of the phantasm is motion in the extra-organic object. In fact, it would be accurate to say that the cause is that set of motions which *is* the extra-organic object. The phantasm itself, as a matter of existence, is motion; but not the motion propagated into the organism without alteration. On the contrary, it is rather the product of the combination or interaction of two motions or two sets of motions. That which forms the content of the sentient's perception is, therefore, a complex of sense qualities; and it is the *joint* product of the extra-organic object and the equally physical living organism. The psychological fact is thus not the "divers motions" of the external object, but another set of "divers motions" differing from the former in two ways: first, in that the latter are *motions in the sentient organism,* and secondly, in that they are the *results* of the former set of motions acting upon, and being reacted upon by, the percipient organism. In other terms, the psychological content is the immediate data of sense; for physics it is the motion accidents of body. A remark of Hobbes's [34] may elucidate the point. The sun, he says, seems to the eye no bigger than a dish: but "there is behind it somewhere something else, I suppose a real sun, which creates these fancies, by working, one way or other, upon my eye, and other organs of my senses, to cause that diversity of fancy." The "real sun" indicates the external object stimulus; the "diversity of fancy," the sun-having-the-size-of-a-dish, is the content of the perception.

We are simply endeavoring here to render clear the difference between the phantasm and its extra-organic correspondent as Hobbes himself saw it. Both phantasm and extra-organic object are physical effects—neither is "mental." But the phantasm is not an exact replica of the "object," for they are two "sets of divers motions," and that set which is *phantasm* differs from the correlated set which is the outside "object" by the extent to which motions native to the sentient fuse with the motions propagated from the external object into the sentient. This is consequently no denial of a correspondence, nor, for that matter, of some degree of similarity, between phantasm and outside object; that which is denied is the exact and complete similarity of phantasm and the object without the sentient. In brief, the fact that motions from without enter a living organism makes a difference to those motions.

In the light of this, the assertion that Hobbes's doctrine has nothing to do with "mental states" seems justified. Phantasms are neither "mental," "spiritual," "psychical," nor are they "states of consciousness." Such terms with their customary and modern connotations are totally inapplicable to a psychology of the type of Hobbes's. Seth[35] affords a curious instance of this misapplication. "The immediate objects of the senses are, Hobbes finds, mere 'phantasms' or 'appearances'—as we should say, states of consciousness, having no existence outside the mind itself . . . the object of sense perception is purely subjective, and totally unlike the real object, which is the cause of the sense appearance." But one is forced to protest that by "appearances," Hobbes does not mean what "state of consciousness, having no existence outside the mind" means for us. "Appearances" for Hobbes are related to the real thing as the image in the mirror to the object mirrored; they do

---

[34] *Decameron Physiologicum,* Vol. 7, pp. 80–81.
[35] *English Philosophers and Schools of Philosophy,* pp. 61–62.

not imply an order of existences of a nature radically different from the objects of which they are the appearances. They are existences, effects, of precisely the same nature as the "real thing."

The image is thus related to the object as effect to cause, as an echo to the sounding body, or as a reflection in a mirror to the source from which ether vibrations spring. Now the question may here be raised: Are not images, these echoes and reflections, *equivalent* to states of consciousness? The answer must obviously depend upon what is the precise meaning here ascribed to "states of consciousness." If we define the phrase as denoting simply *what we are aware of* in the operations of sense, and mean literally that, with no implied reservations and considerations concerning the status of things "in consciousness," or dependent for their existence or for their being experienced "on consciousness," or "having their existence only in the mind"—in short, if the phrase be emptied of all so-called subjectivistic implications, Hobbes's phantasms are states of consciousness. But it is essential that all these qualifications be made. It is easy to imagine that, were Hobbes asked what we are aware of in perceptions, he would regard the question as rather stupid, since every man possessing vision saw colors, and having ears heard sounds—in other words, was aware of images, echoes, reflections, phantasms. If states of consciousness are simply what we are aware of, Hobbes would regard it as trifling to ask if what we are aware of are states of consciousness. On the other hand, had Hobbes been asked if phantasms were "subjective," if they were dependent for their existence on consciousness, or the soul, or the mind; or had he been asked if the nature of phantasms were altered by the fact that some consciousness was aware of them, he would have been sorely puzzled to discover what the question was about. He would probably have looked upon it as on a par with asking if the image in the mirror were altered by the mirroring. Not to labor the point further, we may conclude that such questions almost unavoidably inject into Hobbes's doctrine elements not merely foreign to it, but beyond the ken of its author. The questions as to the adequateness to-day of Hobbes's psychology of perception, of the relation of that psychology to present-day positions, and of whether we should hold that Hobbes's phantasm is all that "state of consciousness" should signify, are very different from the question of what Hobbes did mean to say.

If by "mind," in the statement quoted, Seth intends the subject of sense in Hobbes's meaning of the term, then it is true that appearances have no existence outside the mind itself—but then they are not "states of consciousness." For the subject of sense Hobbes does not call mind or soul or consciousness, but *"some living creature"*—and this is a significant fact. Hobbes's phantasms are what he calls them, store of experience. The manifold of experience is this store of phantasms. It is for Hobbes what the sequence of states of consciousness is for the modern subjectivist.  Hobbes's manifold of experience are states of a living creature, phenomena of motion, but the series of states of consciousness, as the phrase is generally used in later subjectivistic thought, implies a group of conceptions and distinctions which simply did not exist for Hobbes.  It is even unfair to Hobbes to say that his store of phantasms is identical with the sequence of physiological processes or neuroses which in most modern psychology is regarded as paralleling a very dissimilar sequence of psychical states.  It is unfair because it tends to represent Hobbes as reacting against a distinction in orders of existence and as erasing the whole world of the "psychical" in order to maintain the sufficiency of the world of the "physical." The point on which too much insistence can hardly be laid, however, is that such a picture of Hobbes is unhistorical, not founded on Hobbes's own words, and that, therefore, the questions that we have been considering are irrelevant.

The trouble, to repeat, is that subjectivity and objectivity, consciousness, mental states, psychical existences, and the like elements of later psychological and epistemological instruments of terminology are completely beyond the sphere of Hobbes's thought.  The appearances and the real objects can not be subsumed under these categories.  They belong to the one order of existents.  The unlikeness of one to the other is simply the unlikeness of one motion to another, of object to reflected image, and not the unlikeness of a "subjective conscious state" to an "objective real object."

When we inquire concerning Hobbes's position with reference to the cognitive correspondence of idea and thing, we are in danger of forcing his thought into channels foreign to it, if we seek to compel an answer. The danger lies in assuming that the *cognitive* correspondence of idea and thing is at the same time a psychophysical correlation of idea as psychical state with a physiological state (and since the latter is the effect of an extra-organic physical cause, the correlation extends to that of psychical state and physical object).  It is this confusion which is at the bottom of Seth's misinterpretation considered above.  In forcing this meaning upon Hobbes, we should be introducing surreptitiously that very dualism of substances which he has explicitly repudiated.

In terms of Hobbes's psychology, there is no such correlation of psychical idea with object, since there is nothing that is psychical or spiritual or "mental" in this sense of the term.  From the psychological standpoint, the only correspondence that exists is that of effects to causes.  But from the standpoint of knowledge, this relation of cause and effect is the basis of a *cognitive* correspondence.  The experience of the effects affords the opportunity for knowledge of the causes. Therefore, in raising the question of the cognitive correspondence of idea and thing, we are inquiring how Hobbes uses the physical effects in the sentient, that is, the phantasms, in order to arrive at a knowledge of objects, that is, of causes.

Now the mere possession of images is not, according to Hobbes, in itself knowledge. Image-phantasms are more accurately regarded as the occasions and opportunities for cognition than actual cases of knowing. Images afford a certain guidance to the sentient organism in its activities, but are not in themselves knowledge. As physical effects in the all-embracing system of nature, phantasms and images are part of the subject-matter of inquiry rather than the knowing itself. Real knowledge depends on the consistent use of the terms of discourse, and ratiocination is computation involving such consistent manipulation of terms. But the terms must be connected up with objects (which are really causes in the dynamic system of nature) in a scheme of definite correspondence. This is secured through the instrumentality of the image-phantasms.

Now the image-phantasms which make up experience are as varied as their outside causes. The possession of certain phantasms leads to the adoption of a name as a sign of the causes of the phantasm-effects. Thus, as in the illustration cited above, the term "sun" will signify the extra-organic cause of the intra-organic state or phantasm "sun-being-the-size-of-a-dish," and of experiences of a similar nature. The "real sun, which creates these fancies" is the cognitive correlate of the term "sun" which is adopted in order to connect the "diversity of fancy" or phantasms with the "real sun." Through the use of names as signs associated with a given group or kind of phantasms, we are able to discriminate and distinguish the external causes. Thus the cognitive function of phantasms resides not so much in the images themselves (for the image in and by itself is not knowing) as in their capacity to be indices of the extra-organic causes, and in fixation of this causal reference by means of names. The names once fixed, agreed upon, and their reference maintained, ratiocination, or computation by means of names, furnishes knowledge.

It is clear, therefore, that the doctrine of cognitive correspondence in Hobbes is far from any implications of psychophysical dualism. The correspondence, to repeat, is based on the relation of cause and effect. And both cause and effect are of the same order of existence, physical changes in a mechanical system. The similarity of idea (phantasm) and object is a similarity of cause and effect.

In the philosophy of Hobbes, accordingly, plurality of substances is supplanted by a mechanical system of nature. The cognitive correspondence of idea and object, in so far as it means a plurality or duality of substances, has no place in his doctrine. The result is that the problems connected with the contrasts of two realms of existents, the psychical and the physical, of mind and matter, body and soul, of "mental state and object," of the subjective and the objective, simply do not arise. Their absence from his philosophy may, or may not, signify grave deficiencies in his doctrine; its freedom from such problems may indicate its inadequacy. That, however, is not here in question. The point of interest is that, with the rejection of a two-substance theory, there is no occasion for such questions. Indeed, the nature of Hobbes's epistemology is more truly grasped by keeping in mind his conception of nature as a mechanical system of causes and effects than by reference to the doctrine of one substance. For at bottom, as has been intimated, the notion of one substance plays a silent rôle. It is an empty notion for Hobbes, and is really supplanted by the theory of nature. His concern with the notion is derived mainly from the historical importance of the concept of substance. And this much appears from his philosophy, that the notion of a single substance, or more correctly, the new scientific view of nature, as the metaphysical foundation for his developed thought, did not generate for him that order of problems which is characteristic of the doctrine of the duality of substances.

It is our purpose to maintain that the psychology of Spinoza is similar in character to that of Hobbes. This likeness in standpoint is but one instance of the several similarities existing between the thought of the two philosophers. We can not from this infer, however, that Hobbes exerted an important influence upon Spinoza. Kuno Fischer is of the opinion that the influence, if there was any, was indirect.[36] Toennies has painstakingly worked out in detail points of resemblance without, however, satisfactorily establishing the dependence of one on the other.[37]

So far as the similarity in character of their psychologies is to be considered, certain doctrines held in common by the two men would render some degree of influence probable. Hobbes and Spinoza shared the mechanistic view of nature; and for both, the human body and "human nature" were an integral part of nature. For both, the realm of existence was the realm of dynamics and of efficient causes. This is a point of more real similarity than their allegiance to a doctrine of the oneness of substance. For Hobbes, substance was after all a rather empty and unutilizable notion; the dynamical, mechanical character of nature, its systematic uniformity, was far more significant for his work. We may regard substance as meaning for Hobbes just this mechanical system. That is, it was substance as standing for this mechanical system that fructified his thinking. For Spinoza, on the contrary, the mechanical system of nature means the attribute of extension; it is secondary rather than primary; while substance is God,

[36] "Spinoza," *Geschichte der neueren Philosophie,* 1909, Vol. 2, pp. 618–619.
[37] "Studien zur Entwicklungsgeschichte des Spinoza," *Vierteljahresschrift für wissenschaftliche Philosophie,* Vol. 7, 1883.

God or substance is the first principle upon which depends the organic assemblage of concepts that forms adequate knowledge. The common interest of Spinoza and Hobbes in the deductive geometric method really covers a difference of spirit. For Hobbes the importance of the geometrical method is derived from his practical identification of mathematics and dynamics or mechanics. For Spinoza the logically and organically necessary relation and dependence of all other concepts upon the concept of God or substance render the geometrical method the type of all true method. Expressed in a different way, for Spinoza the metaphysical doctrine of the oneness of substance was the beginning and the crowning achievement of knowledge; while for Hobbes it was a metaphysical notion mainly valuable as clearing the way for a mechanistic science of nature.

In a sense, therefore, their psychological principles show similarity because of a common outlook upon the natural world. From this point of identity, however, their philosophies radiate in different directions, determined by significant differences of spirit and purpose. A detailed consideration of the points of agreement and disagreement are not here in place. It is sufficient to indicate briefly that it is not *a priori* improbable that Spinoza's psychology should be in essentials like that of Hobbes's.

# PART II

## SPINOZA

### I

Spinozistic exegesis is complicated by the fact that historical circumstances apparently render necessary the construction of his work as a direct continuation of the thought of Descartes. Exegesis has accordingly been generally eisegesis in terms of Cartesianism. Taken superficially, the setting of Spinoza's work seems to point unmistakably to such a manner of envisaging his development and purpose. Looking forward from the outcome of the Cartesian philosophy, the situation is in effect often summarized as follows: Starting from the dualism of substances, that is, the conception of existence as dual, unity may be attained in several ways. One substance may be regarded as constituting all reality, and the existence of the other substance totally denied. Or one might take one substance "reality" and depress the other to the status of "appearance." Or, finally, the duality of existence marked by the two finite opposed substances might be retained in the field of "appearance," the duality being, at bottom, validated; the truly real is then to be found in a single substance which is neither of the Cartesian finite substances, these latter degenerating to the rank of attributes of the one substance. This would mean that the distinction between finite and infinite substance is pushed to its logical consequences. In any case, Descartes's distinction constitutes a persistent menace to the substantial character of finite substances and to their reality. The distinction represents instability. From this angle of vision, it is easy to assume that any one after Descartes who spoke of attributes of thought and extension, had simply substituted for his term "finite substances" the term "attributes," accepting, as to the rest, the distinction between orders of existence, the verbal change leaving unaffected many of the implications of the duality in existence. Thus it is powerfully suggested that we make Spinoza a Cartesian. His passion for unity and his realization of the problems left by Descartes are to be regarded as leading him to lower the finite substances to the position of attributes of the single real substance, and that in this we have the key to his philosophy.

This may be simple enough, but it is misleading. It presents Spinoza as primarily a sort of apostolic successor of Descartes, the continuer of the Cartesian tradition, and the self-appointed synthesizer of that philosophy.  Descartes's influence on Spinoza, obviously not to be denied, may easily be overestimated, and generally is.  The relation of Spinoza to Descartes is not that implied in describing their relation as one of pupil to master, of disciple to apostle.  In the first place, there exists a difference of spirit, of purpose, and of interest that should not be minimized.  And secondly, the interpretation of the doctrinal sequence, attributed by Windelband to the Hegelian "*Geschichts-konstruktion*," which assigns to Malebranche and the occasionalists the rôle of intermediaries between Descartes and Spinoza, conflicts with the chronological order.  Windelband points out that the letters of Geulincx and the chief work of Malebranche were antedated by Spinoza's *Ethics*.  Spinoza could not have been influenced by the thought of the occasionalists and Malebranche concerning the interaction of substances.[1]  And finally, it is, perhaps, worth noticing that Spinoza's contemporaries do not appear to have regarded him as an outstanding champion of Cartesianism.

According to Windelband, the genesis of Spinoza's doctrine can not be substantially accredited to any one agency—neither the Jewish Cabbalists, nor the "Scholastics of the Jewish Middle Ages," nor to Bruno.  All these movements, as well as the Cartesian, were influential, but not even Descartes can be selected as the predominant agency.  And whatever the pristine determinants were, it was Spinoza's peculiar purposes, aspirations, and genius that vitalized and utilized them.

If we approach Spinoza by way of Cartesianism alone, we immediately land in the midst of perplexities.  Spinoza's philosophy centers in the doctrine of the attributes and of their relation to substance.  If we identify Spinoza's thought attribute with Descartes's finite immaterial substance and the extension attribute with the latter's finite material extended substance—if the only point of difference between them is that implied by "attribute of substance" as contrasted with "finite substance"—then a host of difficulties are imported into the situation.  For Spinoza's parallelism of modes becomes virtually a parallelism of the spiritual or psychical to the material or physical.  Spinoza must then be supposed to have started where Descartes finished, with the irreducible opposition of a spiritual principle to the material principle.  We should be led to assume that Spinoza would accept for the definitions of his attributes the meanings that his putative master assigned to the two finite substances. Spinoza, in consequence, is to be understood as having started with a dualistic view of existence as the presupposition of his philosophy; it must form the unquestioned and incontestable first principle of his thought.  Or stated without reservation, that which for Descartes was a problem, recognized by him as really unsolved in his own speculations, is the point of departure and basis for

[1] Windelband, *Geschichte der neueren Philosophie*, Leipzig 1911, Vol. I, pp. 206–207.

the investigations of Spinoza.  Reducing finite substances to attributes, his task may be taken as the reconciliation in the unity of substance of the opposition left by Descartes between two finite substances.

The mere statement of the consequences following upon this fashion of conceiving the origin and first intention of Spinoza's philosophy is sufficient to throw suspicion upon it.  The existence of Spinoza's *Principles of the Cartesian Philosophy* probably is partly responsible for the habit of judging Spinoza in this light.  But, after all, it is the principles of the *Cartesian* philosophy that he is expounding for his pupil, and we have no warrant to assume that, therefore, it is the single great source of his own thought.  His appendix to the work indicates his independence.

We are here interested in Spinoza's psychology.  Now if the method of interpretation that has just been stated is not erroneous, then inevitably there follow certain assumptions that must be made preparatory to the study of his psychology. If Spinoza's attributes involve the distinction and contrast that Descartes's finite substances signified, his psychology is, and must have been, developed with those contrasts as limiting notions.  Thought, reason, intellect, soul, idea, notion, conception, mind—such terms as these must denote and connote phenomena of spiritual existence, events in what is now an immaterial, spiritual nonextended attribute, or else stand for that attribute itself. The Cartesian antagonism between ideas in a soul substance and extra-organic objects in extended substance (or intra-organic physiological processes) would surge up in Spinoza's thought in quite analogous form.  The demotion of finite substance to attribute would be, in many respects connected herewith, a merely verbal change.  The Cartesian hesitancy about the image—the desire to assign it unconditionally to the body and the constraint to connect it in some manner with the soul —would be duplicated in his successor's thought.  The Cartesian struggle to devise an interaction between the two substances constituting the human being without flagrant contradiction would be expected to recur in Spinoza in the guise of interaction between the attributes; or else a solution would be sought in the direction of the unity of substance.  In short, it is difficult to understand why Spinoza should not have experienced in his psychology precisely the perplexities that haunted Descartes, if Spinozism is correctly depicted as historically and logically an expression of the growth of Cartesianism.  Indeed, one would expect to find the entanglements more vividly sensed, indicated, and combated.  Such an obviously artificial solution of the question of the reciprocal influencing of mind and body as that proffered by Descartes should accordingly be magnified by Spinoza as a crucial point in his predecessor's philosophy, and to be treated distinctively either as a mistaken concession to the tradition of the interaction of a plur-

ality of substances, or else as a suggestion for a solution needing more
elaborate justification. Spinoza, however, can hardly be considered
as having grappled with these problems; on the contrary, he seems
largely to have left them to one side. Little or nothing in his writings
suggests that he felt that these elements of Cartesian teaching were
germane to his own philosophy. His concern with them, wherever such
concern is traceable, is casual, and implies that he did not recognize
them as indigenous to his own philosophic world. The doctrine of two
attributes in relation to one substance might, or might not, have had
advantages over the problem of the relation of two finite substances to
one infinite substance—but this question is pertinent: Would the
transformation of the problem, granting that Spinoza's problem
is just a transformation of that of Descartes, eliminate really or apparently the unsolved questions of the psychology of a being composed
of two so different constituents? If the former doctrine were merely a
restatement of the Cartesian position, the differences being in the main
terminological, Spinoza would probably have shown himself to be
acutely aware of all those quandaries and embarrassments that spring
to the fore when the duality of finite existence is asserted. The conclusion seems to be that, while it would be excessive to deny the influence of the Cartesian philosophy and psychology, such influence is
not what it is generally supposed to be, and further, that we can deny
that Spinoza's philosophy and psychology form a restatement of Cartesian problems and a direct doctrinal continuation of Descartes's
efforts toward synthesis.

The difficulties involved in putting such a construction upon Spinoza
will appear in the sequel. It is to be maintained in this essay that
Spinoza's philosophy in general, and his psychology in particular, can
not be regarded as such a restatement of problems and a later stage in
the evolution of one doctrine. The claim is advanced that Spinoza's
psychology is thoroughly like that of Hobbes, at least in its first intention.
It is, on the whole, as radically "physiological" as that of Hobbes. As was
asserted of the latter, so of Spinoza it is affirmed, that properly speaking
he is not concerned with "mental states," "states of consciousness,"
"spiritual psychical entities," or "immaterial ideas" in a spiritual principle. His psychological terminology is free from implications possessed by that of Descartes. Neither his philosophy nor his psychology is rooted in a doctrine of existence as dual. Nor do his point of
view and his presuppositions force him to this position in metaphysics.
His psychology, consequently, has nothing to do with that doctrine.

This, to repeat, is Spinoza's real psychology. Whatever symptoms
of tendencies toward "spiritualism" may appear in his psychology are
properly to be taken as lapses from his characteristic standpoint. The
extent to which he may have departed from the attitude intrinsic to his

system as a whole, is a matter difficult to estimate, first, because of terminological considerations, and secondly, because it is hard to calculate the extent to which he felt the psychological implications of Descartes's doctrine. And after all, Spinoza is a metaphysician and ethicist rather than a psychologist; the former interests determine the latter, rather than the reverse. Occasional departures from the dominant standpoint may occur in the interests of a purpose other than psychological, but the majority of passages in which a harking back to pure Cartesianism seems latent turn out to have such allusions only because of the initial assumption that the essential in Spinozism is adequately conceived only in connection with the outcome of Descartes's work.

## II

As a preliminary orientation in the study of Spinoza it may be well to enumerate some of the points wherein his work and that of Descartes are similar. Concerning these similarities, however, certain reservations must be made immediately in order to render clear what follows. In the first place, the instances of agreement are not those which are ordinarily asserted; and secondly, as will become evident, the common elements may forcefully suggest, but can not prove, that Cartesian writings are the only source or even the chief source from which Spinoza might have derived just these elements of agreement. For the important accordances were parts of the general philosophical tradition, and the two men may have depended on the same sources. And it is just in respect to those notions which are peculiarly Cartesian innovations that Spinoza shows least agreement. The concepts of substance, of essence, and the mechanical theory of nature, for example, are by no means exclusively Cartesian. The results of this cursory survey of Descartes will indicate that just where Spinoza and Descartes are most in accord there is the least need of assuming the latter as the inspiration of the former. If Descartes's break with tradition turns upon the discovery of the method of doubt, and allied changes, it is at just this point that the line of cleavage between the two systems begins.

We have been at pains to state that Spinoza's problem is not set in terms of the relation of psychical ideas in a spiritual substance to modes of a physical, extended substance. Nor does Spinoza split existence into halves, things of the mind and things of extension. Idea means for Spinoza what essence had denoted in scholastic philosophy. It is a logical entity, and in explicated form and verbally expressed, it is a definition. Now historically speaking, the problem of the relation of essence to existence verged on the commonplace, while the Cartesian problem of relating two finite opposed substances was relatively novel.

It was, accordingly, more natural for Spinoza's metaphysics and epistemology to turn upon the former distinction than the latter—to conceive the correspondence of the order of ideas to the order of things in terms of essence and existence than in terms of spiritual entities in one substance to physical things constituting the modes of another substance.

This both strengthens the considerations which render dubious the envisagement of Spinoza solely from the Cartesian two-substance point of view, and indicates the direction from which a more successful approach may be undertaken. In addition, we are afforded an important clue to the real nature of the Cartesian influence. The *Rules for the Direction of the Mind* comes nearer being the major source of Descartes's influence on Spinoza, or represents more adequately Spinoza's point of departure, than any other of Descartes's writings that we can assign. Spinoza's point of departure, in so far as it is Cartesian at all, or is exemplified in Descartes, is discoverable, not in the final stages of the earlier thinker's work, but in the first stages. It was denied above that the relation of finite substance to infinite substance, and the psychological and epistemological consequences of the dualism, were taken by Spinoza as the kernel of his problem. Now just these elements of Descartes's thought are least apparent in the *Rules for the Direction of the Mind*. A brief consideration of the position developed in this work of Descartes will afford a desirable approach to Spinoza.

In the *Rules for the Direction of the Mind*, as compared with later writings, the dualism of substances had not become a powerful or controlling feature in the writer's thought. The psychological and epistemological consequences of that doctrine were avoided, or else had not been clearly sensed. In this early work Descartes is chiefly concerned with notions closely allied to typical doctrines of scholasticism. This is especially true of his treatment of intuition and "simple natures," "simple truths," or essences. The question of the status of these simples in relation to an immaterial spiritual substantial mind was at least in abeyance, or, more probably, had not arisen. The knowledge problem as stated in the *Rules for the Direction of the Mind* has close affiliations with orthodox scholasticism. The position is consistently maintained that the understanding alone is the knower, while sense, imagination, and memory are "aids" to the understanding in its labors. "Nothing can be known prior to the understanding, since the knowledge of all things else depends upon this and not conversely." When one has "clearly grasped all those things which follow proximately on the knowledge of the naked understanding, he will enumerate among other things whatever instruments of thought we have other than the understanding; and these are only two, *viz.*, imagination and sense. He will, therefore, devote all his energies to the distinguishing and examining of these three modes of cognition, and seeing that in the strict sense truth and falsity can be a matter of the understanding alone, though often it derives its origin from the other two faculties, he will attend carefully to every source of deception in order that he may be on his guard."[1] But these aids are of service only with reference to corporeal things, for if the understanding "deal with matters in which there is nothing corporeal or similar to the corporeal, it can not be helped by those faculties (*i.e.*, sense, memory, and imagination)."[2] Now the true function of understanding in itself, aside from its utilization of sense and imagination, is the discovery or apprehension (intuition) of the simple natures or logical self-evidents (that is, logical essences which are known *per se*), and their deductive ordering.[3] Irreducible mathematical notions are such essences. The essences are, of course, immaterial, in accordance with the typical scholastic position. In knowledge of essences, for Descartes, the activity of understanding is its own spontaneity, for the essences are congeners of an ideal or immaterial thinking principle. The knowing or understanding is thus the grasping of the ideal or immaterial nature of essence. The discernment of such ideal simples is an immediate act which Descartes, at this stage of his development at least, conceives as an immediate apprehension in a logical, not a psychological, sense. When he speaks of the deductive method, which rests upon the intuition of the unanalyzable logical elements as compared with the method of experience, he has in mind a method of ordering logical entities in a deductive scheme comparable to mathematical exposition. Mathematical formulae, in fact, stand for just such logical simples, or the results of thought upon such elementary self-evidents.

In the simple natures there is no falsity[4] and "in order to know these simple natures no pains need be taken, because they are of themselves sufficiently well known. Application comes in only in isolating them from each other and scrutinizing them separately with steadfast mental gaze."[5] Falsity occurs only through the failure to corroborate the results of successive logical steps by intuition and an active use of memory, or through uncritical reliance on the imagination and sense.[6]

This preliminary stage in Descartes's meditations forces a problem upon him that resembles one which Hobbes had to face. Hobbes perceived that the experiential elements upon which knowledge of nature is to be built consist of phantasms and images, which are *effects;* but

[1] *Philosophical Works of Descartes, Rules for the Direction of the Mind.* trans. by Ross and Haldane, Vol. I, pp. 24–25; *cf.* p. 35.
[2] *ibid,* p. 39.
[3] *cf. ibid,* p. 16.
[4] *ibid,* p. 42.
[5] *ibid,* pp. 45–46.
[6] *cf. ibid,* p. 44

reasoning from effects to causes can furnish only conjectural and particular knowledge, and not necessary knowledge. Correspondingly in Descartes, the starting-point is essence, on the one hand, and on the other, the particular sense effects. With reference to a science of nature the mathematical truths of essence, immaterial and ideal, which are known with immediate certainty, are the bases of necessity in such knowledge. A science of nature implies a transition from ideal entities to physical existences.

Descartes's *Rules for the Direction of the Mind*, with which we are here concerned, is hardly more than an unfinished sketch, and contains no complete solution of the problem. But the outlines of such a solution are given. To these outlines we may here confine ourselves, refraining from a consideration of the transformations in the question and solution which may characterize his later thought.

Now the question of a knowledge of nature demands a treatment of the psychology of perception and imagination. Sense and imagination in the *Rules for the Direction of the Mind* are purely properties of the body. The image is the species, now construed as essentially geometrical form, which is propagated, "uncontaminated and without bodily admixture from the external senses," to the fancy or imagination.[7] The perceptual process furnishes an image whose mathematical kinship with the intuited pure logical essence of extension smooths over many difficulties. Because of this kinship, images and sensations can be *subsumed under* the deductions from essences. They are, therefore, at least existential exemplifications of a theoretical necessary conclusion. In so far as a science of nature or physical existences is mathematical in structure, the constitution of the image as a sort of geometrical form facilitates the transition from essence to existence, for the "infinitude of figures suffices to express all the differences in sensible things."[8] Whatever difficulties Descartes found at this time in conceiving the possibility of immediately apprehending the corporeal image were similarly lightened. The function of imagination and sense as the instruments of understanding is thus visible in its correct light. In order, therefore, to have knowledge of existence, there is no necessity for having recourse to particular occurrences, except in order to perceive the correspondence of the deductions from the formulae or essences to the particular modes of extension.

The purpose of this excursus is to portray briefly the doctrine which served as orientating forces in shaping the Spinozistic method and purpose, whether the origin of this influence be exclusively, or in part, or not at all, in Descartes's *Rules for the Direction of the Mind*. In opposition to the customary manner of entering Spinoza's thought

[7] *ibid*, p. 38.
[8] *ibid*, p. 37.

from the dualistic outcome of Descartes, and of ascribing to Spinoza that dualism and its implications as his point of departure, this other, and juster, characterization of Spinoza's point of departure is given. Our denial that Spinoza was a Cartesian refers to the first characterization; the obviously necessary recognition that Descartes must have exerted a directive influence upon Spinoza refers to the second characterization, and suggests what the deeper part of that influence was. It is not claimed, of course, that the *Rules for the Direction of the Mind* was the only source of the Cartesian influence. What is asserted is that the standpoint of this work is more similar to Spinozistic doctrines than most of the Cartesian works; and that if it were without great influence on Spinoza, yet the work reveals, as will appear in the sequel, such a sympathetic philosophical kinship with the latter's position that a direct and fruitful influence is powerfully suggested. On the other hand, with many of the later transformations of Descartes's tenets Spinoza must have been thoroughly at variance. At any rate, we may venture the assertion at the present stage that the approach to Spinoza from this element of Cartesian teaching is a better preparation for the penetration of Spinoza's meaning than the more customary mode of procedure. The complete justification of this assertion, of course, is found only in this essay taken as a whole.

Spinoza himself has given us an exposition of the "Principles of the Cartesian Philosophy." Obviously, as the writer of an exposition of that philosophy, he writes as a Cartesian, since it is Descartes's doctrine that he is expounding. But he has also furnished an *Appendix* to that exposition, in which he purposed to treat, as the sub-title states, of certain general and special difficulties of metaphysics, of being and the affections of being, of God and His attributes, and of the human mind. Here we would naturally expect to discover indications of the precise nature of Descartes's influence on Spinoza, signs of modification in the former's doctrine in Spinoza's reaction to it, and clues to the future development of the latter. The following questions accordingly seem pertinent: What sort of philosophy does Spinoza offer in the *Cogitata Metaphysica?* What evidence does it afford that Spinoza attacks his problems from the standpoint of the outcome of Cartesian thought, and to what extent are Cartesian elements conscious or unconscious presuppositions for Spinoza? What independence and original interest does the work reveal? In other words, are such later Cartesian elements as the duality of existence, the psychologically spiritual nature of the idea, and the spiritualistic trend of Cartesian psychology with its reflex influences on his epistemology and metaphysics, reproduced by Spinoza as accepted doctrines or tacit assumptions?

The briefest answer to these questions is this: the *Cogitata Metaphysica,* in standpoint and spirit, is more closely affiliated with the leading ideas of the *Rules for the Direction of the Mind* than with any other Cartesian work. Spinoza impresses the reader as interpreting the Cartesian conceptions of the *Principles* in the light of notions analogous to, if not derived from, the principles of the *Rules for the Direction of the Mind.*

The poles of the thought of the *Cogitata Metaphysica* are essences, on the one hand, and existences, on the other—a logically organized system of essences forming knowledge and a causally determined and mechanically organized world or nature. Essences are logical entities, and just that. If we inquire what we mean by essence, we are referred to definition, for every definition explicates the essence of something.[9] Knowledge is wholly a matter of essences, and memory, imagination, and, presumably, sense are devices, instrumental in attaining knowledge, but no more than for Descartes in the *Rules for the Direction of the Mind* are they in themselves cognitive.[10] Their serviceableness appears when Spinoza confronts this difficulty: The formal essence has neither been created nor does it exist by itself, but it depends on the divine essence; the essences of things are eternal. How, then, can we, in the absence of adequate knowledge of the nature of God, the final ground of all explanation, know the essences of things? Spinoza's answer is that knowledge of the essences of things is possible because things are already created. If this were not the case, knowledge of things would be impossible except after adequate knowledge of the nature of God. Analogously, if we were ignorant of the nature of a parabola, it would be impossible to know the nature of its orderly applications. Spinoza's thought may be rendered in this way: true knowledge of existence is knowledge of essence; from an adequate knowledge of the supreme essence, God, knowledge of all essences would follow. But since we do not possess such perfect knowledge, we must avail ourselves of the fact that created things exist as actualized essences, and through experience of the *esse existentiae* arrive at the perception of the essence. Sense and imagination facilitate the process; they are occasions for, and auxiliary instrumentalities in, the process of cognizing the essence, while the actual apprehension of the essence through experience of the factual exemplars is the function of understanding or reason alone. Imagination and memory are, accordingly, in Spinoza's language, mere *entia rationis*, or modes of thinking, which enable us more easily to retain, explain, and represent things of the mind (*res intellectas*).[11] And knowledge as the system of apprehended essences relates to understanding alone.

The mechanical theory of nature, sponsored by Descartes, is advo-

[9] *cf. Cogitata Metaphysica*, Pt. 1, ch. 2, p. 193. All references to the works of Spinoza, unless otherwise specified, are to the Van Vloten and Land edition of the Opera, 3rd edition, 1914.
[10] *Cogitata Metaphysica*, Pt. 1, ch. 1, p. 188.
[11] *cf. ibid*, Pt. 1, ch. 1, p. 188; ch. 2, p. 192.

cated by Spinoza. Existence, the world, *natura naturata*—all these terms express the same thing—is a mechanical system. In matter there is "nothing beyond mechanical textures and operations."[12] Had we sufficient knowledge, we would find everything in the order of nature as necessary as that which mathematics teaches.[13] *Natura naturata* is only one single thing, and man is a part of nature, and as such a part must cohere with other parts.[14] It is significant that Spinoza does not say that man's body is a part of nature, but that *man* is a part of nature. He is subject to causal law, either as external cause or as internal cause.[15]

The assertion that the *Cogitata Metaphysica* does not ratify the Cartesian duality of finite existence may encounter the obvious reply that Spinoza does speak of more than one substance; that he divides created substances into extension and thought.[16] But terminological identities are compatible with dissimilarities of meaning. In the first place, it is to be remarked that Spinoza uses the term "substance" loosely; it is clear that he has in mind what later on he signifies by attribute. But a more significant observation is this: he uses the terms *"cogitatio"* and *"mens humana"* for the created thought substance, and *"mens increata"* for the divine thought. Uppermost in Spinoza's mind is the relation of thought to essence. This uncreated mind, or divine thought, is the system of essences (which in God can not be separated from existence). The created thought substance, or *mens humana*, is that kind of being called *esse ideae*—being in so far as it is contained objectively (*objective*) in the idea of God.[17] The spiritualistic and psychological connotations of Descartes's thinking substance are in the main neglected. The only place in the *Cogitata Metaphysica* in which Spinoza seems to recognize these implications is in the last paragraph of the work, where we meet for the only time the contrast between *res corporeales* and *res spirituales*. One may admit that Spinoza may be oscillating between the interpretation of thought substance as subjective essence (essences as knowledge), and as a spiritual, immaterial, soul substance, with an existential status and possessing self-consciousness. But summarizing the tendencies of the *Cogitata Metaphysica*, it is unmistakable that the drift of Spinoza's reflection is away from the latter interpretation. This movement, as we shall see, is completed definitely in the *Ethics*.

In short, in the *Cogitata Metaphysica*, as in the *Rules for the Direction of the Mind*, essence is a logical entity, its incorporeality relates to the ideality of form and not to the spirituality of an existential soul sub-

12 *ibid*, Pt. 2, ch. 6, p. 212.
13 *ibid*, Pt. 2, ch. 6, p. 218.
14 *ibid*.
15 *ibid*, ch. 4, p. 209.
16 *ibid*, Pt. 2, ch. 1, p. 203.
17 *ibid*, Pt. 1, ch. 2, p. 192.

stance, and knowledge rests upon logically immediate self-evidence. Knowledge of essences is a science of ideal forms; the science of nature or existence is a science of hypotheses involving motion, divisibility, and causal necessity. The fundamental distinction is between essence and existence. The division of being into real entities and mental entities (*entia realia* and *entia rationis*) Spinoza repudiates as a bad division.[18] The true division of being is into being which necessarily exists, or whose essence necessarily involves existence, and being whose essence does not involve existence except in possibility.[19] Mental beings —*entia rationis*—are looked upon without any notion of spiritual immateriality. In an important passage he says that *entia rationis* outside the mind (*extra intellectum*) are pure nothing: but if by the term is signified the modes of thinking (*modi cogitandi*) themselves, they are real entities. "For when I ask: what is a *species?* I ask after nothing else than the nature of the mode of thinking itself, which is indeed a being, and is distinguished from another mode of thinking. But these modes of thinking can not be called ideas, nor can they be said to be true or false, just as love can not be called true or false, but only good or bad."[20] When this is connected with what Spinoza writes just before about imagination and memory as modes of thinking, and their identification with movements of the (animal) spirits in the brain, it becomes evident that *entia rationis* or *modi cogitandi* are existences like the human body, and as operations of the human being are part of the order of nature. Essences as knowledge entities, that is *esse ideae*, have no existential status at all, and to inquire concerning such a status is illegitimate because it assumes that they are existences. And, above all, is it significant that Spinoza enumerates intellect itself as one of these modes of thought that is a real entity.[21]

It was pointed out above that it was more natural, with reference to Spinoza's whole philosophical inheritance, for him to conceive metaphysical and epistemological problems in terms of essence and existence than in terms of a finitely irreducible duality of incommutable substances. The excursus into the thought of the *Cogitata Metaphysica*, a work which emanates from an early phase of the philosopher's meditations, has shown that essence and existence were the foci of his thought at that period, and that Spinoza seems on the whole to have interpreted, with conscious intent or otherwise, Descartes's *Principles* in terms of this ancient contrast. It is the purpose of this essay to demonstrate that Spinoza's thought was faithful in its development to this beginning. Spinoza's terminology was undoubtedly affected by the Cartesian, and this has been a help in misleading the historian. The

18 *ibid*, Pt. 1, ch. 1, p. 189.
19 *ibid*, p. 190.
20 *ibid*, Pt. 1, ch. 1, p. 189.
21 *ibid*, Pt. 1, ch. 1, p. 188.

term "idea" was for scholasticism preferably used of ideas in the mind of God. Descartes comes to use it of ideas in the finite mind substance, and signifies by it not only the logical concept, innate ideas, but also at times any "psychological state." He was led to this departure from medieval usage through the reduction of the plurality of substances to a duality. For it is hardly doubtful that for Descartes the finite soul substance was more nearly a congener of the divine substance than was finite extended substance. The doctrine of innate ideas and the onto-logical argument, when stripped of their formal elements, depend upon the awakening of the soul to its own finiteness and imperfection; and the germination of this thought is the necessary implication of the budding comprehension of a perfect being. The enlightenment of the mind is primarily just this discovery of the correlative notions of the perfection of the infinite being and the imperfection of the finite being. Now such a process connotes a certain peculiar intimacy between soul and God. This insight is the divinity of the finite mind. Thus the ap-plication of the term "idea" to at least some of the notions possessed by the finite mind in the dawning of rational comprehension is rendered facile by this implied relationship between finite and infinite mind sub-stance. The widening of the field of usage of the term comes with the acceptance of the psychological consequences of the dualism of sub-stances in the special form of the relation of two substances in one human being. So Spinoza's wider usage of the term may be ascribable to Cartesian example. The *esse ideae* means the being of essence as known or cognized or comprehended, as object of the (finite) mind. But if this account is accurate, new light is thrown upon the legitimacy of the common "Cartesian" interpretation of Spinoza, and upon Spinoza's interpretation of Descartes. For Spinoza, in accepting certain rela-tively novel terminological usages of Descartes, does not necessarily accept every such usage and all the Cartesian implications of terms. For the new application of the term "idea" in Descartes, shared by Spinoza whether derived from Descartes or not, retroactively facili-tates Spinoza's understanding of Descartes as primarily concerned with essence, and helps to explain his neglect of, or indifference to, the spiritualistic psychological connotations of the term in his pre-decessor's writings.

The kinship of the *Cogitata Metaphysica* and the *Rules for the Direc-tion of the Mind* in their outlook upon problems is evident. As has been observed above, we are not here concerned with demonstrating important influences of the *Rules for the Direction of the Mind* upon Spinoza. It would be an exceedingly difficult matter to corroborate such a claim. The point of interest is that the starting-points of both thinkers contained striking similarities, and that a more ade-quate conception of their work is provided when we view them as pursuing divergent paths, as they carry out their work, although starting from similar beginnings, rather than by involuting Spinoza's doctrine with the Cartesian speculations as a later stage of one development.

Spinoza proceeds from the *Cogitata Metaphysica* without signal deviations from the general position therein indicated. Descartes, on the other hand, does change in more than one momentous way from the thought scheme of the *Rules for the Direction of the Mind*. Within the limits of this essay these differences can only be summarized. Descartes's test of truth in this work is logical immediacy, the self-evidence of the logical entity or simple nature. To this Spinoza subscribes and to this he holds fast. But Descartes switches over to psychological immediacy, the certainty of the self-conscious soul in its awareness of its own states. The duality of existence, the spiritualistic psychology, influence, and are influenced by, the acute problems of teleology and mechanism, freedom and determinism, and personal immortality. Spinoza calmly accepts the consequences of the new science of nature, and passes on to doctrines concerning freedom, immortality, and teleology that could hardly have been other than exasperating and heretical to a true Cartesian. In the interplay of forces that drove Descartes to the new positions, the duality of existence emerges, more significant as result than as cause. Spinoza either escapes these forces, or does not succumb to them, or finally may have remained insusceptible to many considerations that were vital to other men of his day because they were uncongenial to his native interests. He is not driven to the doctrine of existence as dual, nor does the doctrine, through the mediation of Descartes, affect him more than superficially. And there is good reason for saying that Spinoza never fully realized what the issues that resulted from the duality of substances really implied. In short, Spinoza was never truly a Cartesian.

### III

Having thus outlined the approach and the point of view from which this study is undertaken, it behooves us to present Spinoza's doctrine in more detailed and positive fashion. The introductory remarks and the contentions therein outlined will be justified, it is hoped, by the results of an investigation free from the customary Cartesianism of the interpretations of the majority of commentators and historians. In showing the exact character of Spinoza's problem and the traits of his attempted solution, we shall first sketch the leading features of his doctrine concerning ideas and existence; after which will be considered his account of the idea and the image from the standpoint of psychology, attending in some detail to the difficulties that result from injecting Cartesian meanings into his terminology.

Since Spinoza is so often hailed as the first "parallelist," part of the task will be to vindicate the claim that neither "parallelism" nor "interactionism" in their common acceptation can legitimately be applied to this philosophy; that his teaching is not characterized by "spiritualistic" tendencies derived from the Cartesian demarcation of two contrasted fields of existence; and that the application of such terms to this philosophy imports alien meanings into all of Spinoza's speculations.

We begin with the essay *On the Improvement of the Understanding* and the account of knowledge and method there suggested.

Knowledge is the possession of true ideas. All the modes of knowledge may be reduced to four. The fourth and highest kind is the perception arising "when a thing is perceived through its essence alone, or through the knowledge of its proximate cause."[1] This mode alone "comprehends the adequate essence of a thing without danger of error."[2] But what is a true idea? We are informed first of all that it is "something different from its correlate (*ideatum*)."[3] Secondly, it is "capable of being understood through itself."[4] The phrase "understood through itself" is pregnant with meaning, and that meaning reveals Spinoza's position. It signifies that the idea, as logical essence, has its place in a deductively ordered system, and bears to other essences the relation of superordination or subordination. "The idea, in so far as its formal essence (*essentia formalis*) is concerned, may be the object of another subjective essence (*essentia objectiva*). And again this second subjective essence will, regarded in itself, be something real and intelligible; and so on, indefinitely."[5] The signification of another characteristic Spinozistic phrase, "*idea ideae*," the idea of an idea, expresses this same systematic arrangement of concepts.

The adequate idea is the true idea; and the adequate idea is "the subjective essence (*essentia objectiva*) of a thing."[6] Finally, "the subjective essence of a thing and its certainty are one and the same."[7] Evidently, then, to have true knowledge is to possess true or adequate ideas (*essentia objectiva*) and to have such ideas is in itself to have certainty and to be assured of certainty.

From this it follows that certainty does not depend on the establishment of relations between ideas and things and the determination of the precise nature of such relations; the test of the validity of an idea is not in the correspondence of the idea and the thing. Method is not concerned with the derivation of ideas from the experiences of fact. "As for this reason (*i.e.*, that the subjective essence involves

[1] Vol. I, p. 7.
[2] *ibid*, p. 10.
[3] *ibid*, p. 11.
[4] *ibid*, p. 10.
[5] *ibid*, p. 11.
[6] *ibid*, p. 12.
[7] *ibid*, p. 12.

certainty) the truth needs no sign—it being sufficient to possess the subjective essences of things, or, what amounts to the same, ideas, in order that all doubts may be removed—it follows that the true method . . . is the order in which we should seek for truth itself, or the subjective essences of things, or ideas, for all these expressions are synonymous." [8] Certainty is thus inherent in the logical essences and is not to be established by reference to what is extrinsic to them. Method is, therefore, a question of the apprehension of the logical certainty of an idea and of its involution in a system of logical concepts. "Method ought necessarily to be concerned with reasoning or understanding: that is, method is not identical with reasoning in order to understand the causes of things, still less is it the comprehension of the causes of things; but it is to understand what a true idea is by distinguishing it from other perceptions and by investigating its nature, in order that we may know our power of understanding." [9] "Method is nothing else than reflective knowledge, or the idea of an idea." [10]

But if truth, as Spinoza says, "makes itself manifest," method must contain principles of guidance, or tests, by means of which the true idea can be disentangled from the welter of fictions, inadequate ideas, chimeras, and false ideas. The surmounting of this difficulty pivots on the distinction between essence and existence. "Every perception is either of a thing considered as existing, or of the essence alone. Now 'fiction' is chiefly concerned with things considered as existing."[11] Error, in general, can not arise from the logical essence, for that would be equivalent to error arising from truth, but only from its obscuration by, or its concealment beneath, the foreign accretions imported from the experiences of the particulars of existence. In a word, "ideas fictitious, false, and the rest, originate in the imagination." [12] Now as we shall see later, the Spinozistic conception of imagination is purely physiological in nature. The operations of the imagination "whereby the effects of imagination are produced, take place according to other laws quite different from the laws of the understanding." We fall into "grave errors through not distinguishing accurately between the imagination and the understanding."[13] "Ideas fictitious, false, and the rest" (that is, in general, all error) originate in the imagination, that is, in "certain sensations, fortuitous (so to speak) and disconnected, which do not arise from the power of the mind itself, but from external causes, according as the body, sleeping or waking, receives various motions." [14] Words are a great source

[8] ibid, p. 12.
[9] ibid, p. 12, italics mine.
[10] ibid, p. 12.
[11] ibid, p. 15.
[12] ibid, p. 26.
[13] ibid, p. 27.
[14] ibid, p. 26.

of error, but words are a part of the imagination. Words lead to error when we form conceptions that are occasioned by confusions in memory because of certain bodily conditions. Words, since they are formed at the caprice of the vulgar, are signs of things as they are in imagination, not as they are in the understanding. Here we find the characteristic distinction between the facts of imagination and the ideas of the understanding.[15] And error results from the failure to discriminate between the two. Imagination, it is clear, is the instrument through which the experience of particular existences is made possible; if the presentations from imagination of particular existences be selected as the source of knowledge, we shall be deceived. For the true knowledge of things is derived not from the imaginative representation (itself an existent, a thing) of particular existents, but from the unalloyed concept or essence. For this reason the confusion of essence and existence was called the pivotal point in the treatment of error.

The resolution of the problem amounts to this: the true idea is simple, clear, and distinct, and carries within itself the principle by which its certainty is made manifest: the fiction, the inadequate idea, and in general all falsities are deficient in one or all of these respects. "A true idea (*cogitatio*) is distinguished from a false one, not so much by its extrinsic mark (*denominatio*), but most of all by its intrinsic mark . . . there is in ideas something real, whereby the true are distinguished from the false. . . For thought is said to be true, if it involves subjectively (*objective*) the essence of any principle which has no cause, and is known through itself and in itself. Wherefore the reality (*forma*) of true thought must be situated in that thought itself, without reference to other thoughts: nor does it acknowledge the object as its cause, but must depend on the very power and nature of the understanding." [16] Understanding in itself, therefore, is able to establish the truth and reality of its thought. The devoted mind, possessed of true insight and correct method, can find within itself the guarantee of the validity of its ideas. This is an expression of Spinoza's rationalistic faith.

Let us ask: What is the "object aimed at"? and What are the "means of its attainment"? As to means, we learn that everything must be conceived "either through its essence alone or through its proximate cause." [17] The true method of discovery is to "form thoughts from some given definition," and a definition, we note, "must explain the inmost essence of a thing." [18]

If definition, expressing the inmost essence of a thing, that is, the

---

[15] *cf. ibid*, p. 27.
[16] *ibid*, p. 22.
[17] *ibid*, p. 28.
[18] *ibid*, p. 29.

truly logical definition, is the means, what is the object aimed at? It is "the acquisition of clear and distinct ideas, such as are made by the pure intellect (*mens*) and not by chance motions of the body." The distinction between imagination and understanding evidently underlies this statement.[19] In a word, the goal is completely unified knowledge. But the peculiar meaning of such knowledge for Spinoza must be determined. "In order that all ideas may be reduced to one," Spinoza asserts, we must so "associate and order them that our mind may, as far as it can, report subjectively (*objective*) the reality of nature, both as whole and as parts."[20] But in an ordered system of essences, there must be some principle which contains in itself the secret of that order, coherence, and unity. "In order that our mind may report wholly . . . the image of nature, our mind should draw out all its ideas from the idea which represents the origin and source of the whole of nature."[21] This first great idea, the architectonical principle of the system of essences as forming knowledge, we shall discover to be the idea of God or Substance. "We should inquire whether there be any being . . . that is the cause of all things, so that its essence, represented in thought (*objective*), may be the cause of all our ideas: and then our mind will to the utmost possible extent represent nature; for it will possess, subjectively, nature's essence, order, and union."[22]

Now the expressions "cause of ideas" and "cause of things" bring into consideration the attributes, thought, and extension. The term "cause" is used in two meanings, dependent upon the distinction between the attributes. The attribute of thought is nothing but the series of ideas or logical essences arranged in logical sequence. "Cause" as referring to this series has a purely logical meaning, expressing the subordination of concepts. One idea causes another in the sense that the concept of a circle is the cause of certain other ideas, those of the properties of a circle, which can be deduced therefrom. The attribute of extension comprises the series of physical things, or simply, things. With respect to this series, the term "cause" has the ordinary scientific meaning, the conditions of the existence of a given thing.

All things, the sum total called nature, as comprehended under the attribute of extension, are existences. But as comprehended under the attribute of thought, they are not existences—they do not *exist*, but they are *known*. For the attribute of thought is the series of essences or pure concepts. It is meaningless to ask whether the essences exist. Knowledge, therefore, is the apprehension of things under the attribute of thought, that is, as essences. And just as the

[19] *cf.* Spinoza's note.
[20] *ibid*, p. 28.
[21] *ibid*, p. 13.
[22] *ibid*, p. 30.

causal nexus of existence is a processus from God or Substance, so the logical nexus of essences is a processus from God or Substance. True progress of the understanding requires, accordingly, the contemplation of the "series of fixed and eternal things" (the essences), not the "series of particular and mutable things." Of the latter, Spinoza says that "their existence has no connection with their essence, or . . . is not eternal truth. Neither is there any need that we should understand their series, for the essences of particular mutable things are not to be gathered from their series or order of existence, which would furnish us with nothing beyond their extrinsic denominations, their relations, or, at most, their circumstances . . . these mutable particular things depend so intimately and essentially . . . upon the fixed things, that they can not either be or be conceived without them." [23]

We are now in a position to understand aright what is meant by the assertion that the "order and connection of ideas is the same as the order and connection of things." This parallelism has no implication of psychophysical parallelism. What is intended by Spinoza is a statement of the correlation of logical essence and thing, between the definition or explanation of a thing and the thing itself. There is but one existential series, that of material things. If our concept system of knowledge is true, if it *is* knowledge of actuality, then the order and connection of ideas must be the same as the order and connection of things. That is, existence contains exemplars, actualizations of the essences, or of some of them at least. All that exists and is actual illustrates, conforms to, and bodies forth some essence. It is necessary to refrain from identifying the "existence" of Spinoza with the "physical" half of the contrast between the spiritual and the material. That is, our conception of what Spinoza intends by existence must be strictly divorced from any connection with the connotations of the dualistic view of existence. In the light of the fact that Spinoza has little or nothing to say concerning "spiritual" existences, we have no warrant for assuming the dual view as the contextual setting of his notion of the existential. To assert that the existential series is the world of the physical, the corporeal, or of "matter" is apt to introduce furtively just that distinction between two fields of existence which we are here concerned to prove foreign to Spinoza. It is likely, at least, to project his utterances upon such a background that he will appear to be reacting against the notion of spiritual existence and is interested in denying such existence and in affirming that all existence is corporeality. The meaning of a Cartesian finite substance is more amply elucidated when each is utilized in turn as the setting of the other. But it is not being scrupulously exact when we adopt such a procedure with Spinoza.

[23] *ibid*, p. 34.

Whether Spinoza's true position *amounts to the same thing* as asserting that all existence is matter, is one thing; but whether he was
consciously interested in limiting existence to "matter" and in denying
psychical or spiritual existence, is a very different thing.  With the
first we have at present no concern; as for the second, it seems more
faithful to Spinoza's development, meaning, and purposes to represent him as being largely indifferent to the spiritual-physical contrast
and as having remained for the most part aloof from the history of
the dualism in Cartesian circles.  When we seek to identify Spinoza's
existential series with the notion of extended substance or with the
modern conception descending from the Cartesian idea, we are virtually regarding a reaction against the splitting-up of existence into
two opposed realms as helping to determine his course of thought.
And it is not easy then to avoid a feeling that it was his rebound from
that notion that eventuated in a limiting of existence to the one type.
To repeat, that may be, in effect, what Spinoza does: but it is not why
he does it.  Unbiassed elucidation of his doctrine requires that we
take the notions of essence and existence as the first terms in which
he thought without attempting to identify this distinction with a set of
ideas of different complexion.

The correspondence of the order and connection of things to the
order and connection of ideas is then a statement of the fact that for
every existence there is an essence, discovered or discoverable, which
is the truth of that existence, its explanation, definition—its law.
Existence is governed by causal necessity; knowledge of existence is
regulated by logical necessity.  That which exists actually, exists
necessarily; that which is thought with necessity is true.  But we
must not look for the order and connection in a cross-section of the
series, but longitudinally as being derived from substance.  There are
two nexi: one causal, and of things, of actuality; the other logical,
in verbal form a series of propositions.  Both are derived from substance.  Consider the statement: "I said that God is the cause of an
idea—for instance, of the idea of a circle—in so far as he is a thinking
thing, simply because the actual being of the idea of a circle can only
be perceived as a proximate cause through another mode of thinking,
and that again through another, and so on to infinity; so that, as
long as we consider things as modes of thinking, we must explain the
order of the whole of nature, or the whole chain of causes, through the
attribute of thought only."[24]  This does not mean that God causes an
idea (psychical or otherwise) in the usual sense of cause, but that God
is the cause of the idea of the circle in the same sense as that the
circle is the "cause" of certain other ideas which are geometrical deductions from and consequences of the idea of a circle.  The chain of

[24] *Ethics*, Pt. 2, p. 7, note.

natural, actual, causes corresponds to a sequence of propositions whose connections are logical; and if God or substance is the origin of the causal series, he is similarly the first principle, the source of coherence and order, in the logical series. The correspondence of idea and thing is comparable to the correspondence of the concept of a curve as expressed in the equation of the curve to that curve as actually existing or as described by a moving object.[25]

A brief consideration of Spinoza's classification of ideas and the treatment of error will substantiate our thesis. The distinction between kinds and classes of ideas corresponds to the various kinds or degrees of knowledge. Three kinds of knowledge are enumerated— knowledge of imagination, or opinion, knowledge of reason, and knowledge of intuition. The first is knowledge based on confused or inadequate ideas, the two latter form knowledge of adequate and true ideas. Now it is noteworthy that these distinctions are based on logical, not psychological, considerations, and give evidence that Spinoza's scheme is logical.

The test of the fictitious idea is logical. The chimera is a fiction the nature of which implies contradiction.[26] Fictions in general are concerned only with the possible—that is, with things whose existence or non-existence would not imply a contradiction.[27] All fictitious ideas are deficient with respect to clearness and distinctness and simplicity, while the adequate idea, the logical essence, possesses just these qualities. All these signs by which we can detect the fictitious or confused ideas are logical qualities. And the same is true of the false idea, which "only differs from the fictitious idea in the fact of implying a mental assent." [28]

Now all falsity consists in "the privation of knowledge, which inadequate, fragmentary, or confused ideas involve." [29] Falsity is due to nothing positive in ideas; [30] it is due to an inadequacy, for the adequate idea is always true. [31] "All confusion arises from the fact that the mind has only partial knowledge of a thing . . . and does not distinguish between the known and the unknown." [32] And fictitious and false ideas are confused ideas. Thus, this confusion is the result of a privation in knowledge—or it may be called that privation itself.

The point involved can be rendered as follows: the simple logical essence necessarily has its correlate in existence either actually or potentially. But the simple, adequate idea may be obscured by the pre-

[25] cf. De Intellectus Emendatione, p. 33.
[26] De Intellectus Emendatione, p. 17.
[27] ibid, p. 16.
[28] ibid, p. 22.
[29] Ethics, Pt. 2, prop. 35.
[30] ibid, prop. 33.
[31] ibid, prop. 34.
[32] De Intellectus Emendatione, p. 20.

sentations of imagination, or the attainment of the idea hampered by the commingling of images and the pure concept. The image is the product of two factors: the external stimulating "object" and the organism itself.[33]

Now while everything that happens in nature, happens of necessity, we can not always be sure that the conjunction of circumstances necessary for the production of the given event actually occurs. The possibilities of such conjunctions, that is, the possibility of the thing's existence, must be ascertained from a scrutiny of the essence; its actuality can only be observed by "attending to the order of nature." Imagination is the instrument for knowledge of the occurrence of particular and mutable things. It is this latter type of knowledge which is subject to error; and in so far as the presentations of imagination prevent, or hinder, the work of understanding, or obscure the logical essence through alloying it with such presentations, we have error, fiction, and falsity. The images themselves, which are themselves existents, do not contain error. "The mind does not err in the mere act of imagining, but only in so far as it is regarded as being without the idea." [34] The presentations of imagination are confused and indistinct (in a logical sense, not psychologically). The concept or essence is distinct and necessarily true, since it has its correlate in actuality. It is not, therefore, the indistinctness of the imagination itself that is the source of error, but the confusion that results from failing to discriminate between the concept and the images. The concept, so to speak, is embedded in a mass of images of the manifold; the idea in its simplicity and clearness is not given, but must be attained. Once attained, its true and necessary existence is given. In so far as we have not attained the concept in its clearness and distinctness, to that extent we are deficient in knowledge, and are correspondingly in danger of error. Privation means deficiency with respect to something that belongs to the nature of the essence in the totality of its logical connections. Thus, I may have the idea of the circle, but I may not know the relation of the diameter to the circumference, and to that extent there is privation or deficiency in my knowledge, on account of which I may be led to make false affirmations. With further development of the understanding, this deficiency is eliminated.

The fictitious, false, and inadequate ideas are logical confusions. The deficiency and confusion concern the logical, not the psychological, structure of the idea. Knowledge of the imagination, or opinion, is concerned with the presentations of particular and mutable things by the imagination; while knowledge of reason and of intuition is knowl-

[33] cf. Ethics, Pt. 2, props. 15 et seq.
[34] Ethics, Pt. 2, prop. 17, note.

edge of the pure concept or essence freed from the trammels of the empirical manifold.

True knowledge, which is knowledge of logical essences, is contrasted with that information of the manifold of experience which we attain through imagination. This contrast corresponds to a contrast in methods. For the method peculiar to the knowledge of essence is to be distinguished from that connected with the investigation of the flux of natural experience. In response to the questions of "J. B." concerning the possibility of a method by means of which we can attain knowledge of the "most excellent things," and whether our mind is ruled by fortune rather than by art, Spinoza replies that "there must necessarily be a method whereby we are able to direct and concatenate our clear and distinct perceptions," and that "the mind is not, like the body, subject to chance." The only support needed for this, he avers, is the following consideration: "One clear and distinct perception, or several such taken together, can be absolutely the cause of other clear and distinct perceptions. Furthermore, all the clear and distinct perceptions, which we form, can arise only from other clear and distinct perceptions, which are in us, nor do they admit of any other cause without us. Whence it follows that clear and distinct perceptions which we form depend upon the certain and fixed laws of our nature alone, that is, on our absolute power, not on fortune." [35] It is evident that clearness and distinctness are logical characteristics of the moments of a pure, logical power of apprehension or mental vision. The clear and distinct perception of the concept of a square "causes" (and this alone can cause) the clear and distinct perception of (say) the incommensurability of diagonal and side. Spinoza has no intention of freeing the "soul" from the vicissitudes of chance by raising it above the causes which "although acting by certain and fixed laws, are yet unknown to us." He is pointing to the fact of the mind's rational insight and its power of inference, and emphatically asserting his confident belief in the existence of a method whereby that capacity can operate successfully. In fact, it is easy to imagine Spinoza selecting geometry as vindicating his claim that there must be such a method and as illustrating his point that clear and distinct perceptions cause, and that they alone can cause, other clear and distinct perceptions. It is here, indeed, that the geometrical method is seen in its true significance. The geometrical method derives its importance for Spinoza from the fact that from his conception of the ordered system of essences flows a demand for such a method. His philosophical task, as viewed by him, points to a method, the most obvious example of which is to be found in geometry.

Spinoza now proceeds to tell what the true method is and to contrast

[35] Vol. 3, Epistola 37.

it with the method applicable to the study of the manifold of experience. "As for other perceptions, I admit that they depend in the largest part on fortune. Hence clearly appears, what the true method ought to be like, and what it ought especially to consist in—namely, solely in the cognition of the pure understanding, and its nature and laws. In order to acquire this, it is before all things necessary to distinguish between the understanding and the imagination, or between true ideas and the rest, such as the fictitious, the false, the doubtful, and absolutely all which depend solely on the memory. For understanding these matters, as far as the method requires, there is no need to know the nature of the mind through its first cause; it is sufficient to put together a short history of the mind, or of perceptions, in the manner taught by Verulam." [36] The method of Bacon for empirical experience, but for final truths, the discernment of the logical essences in their eternal relation to their first cause, substance—this seems to be Spinoza's meaning.

From this it is clear that Spinoza's theory of knowledge does not involve psychological considerations of the relations of idea and object. The problems that cluster about the correspondence of the psychical idea and the physical object are simply outside his universe of discourse. His classification of ideas and knowledge does not arise from the psychological characteristics of mental states, but from the logical properties of the idea.

## IV

After this exposition of Spinoza's doctrine, let us turn specifically to the psychological analyses. We may thereby ascertain to what extent, if at all, Spinoza advocates a psychology in which the notion of the "psychical" or the "spiritual" (taking these terms in the sense of the usual contrast) plays a part. And if the outcome prove that the concept of the psychical or spiritual does not control his psychological opinions, we may then seek confirmation of our theses in a negative way by enumerating some of the difficulties that ensue when the concept is forced upon him. The primary task in the discussion before us is to examine the treatment of the idea and image, and their relation, from the standpoint of psychology.

We may, therefore, begin with idea and image. A distinction between them runs through Spinoza's philosophy, and is as characteristic and as necessary as the corresponding distinction in Descartes; but Spinoza seems to maintain the distinction more consistently. The question inevitably arises in an effort to free the interpretation of Spinoza from the Cartesian meanings read into Spinoza's words,

[36] ibid.

whether, that is, the distinction between image and idea in Spinoza is one and the same as the distinction in Descartes. Does the verbal identity express an identity of meaning?

Now the differentiation of image and idea, of understanding (thinking) and imagination, is, in Descartes, directly connected with the dualism of finite substances in the less general form of the dualism of mind and body in the human being. In fact, the contrast between image and idea in Descartes turns on the difference between the immaterial soul state and the bodily state. Idea signifies something in, or an act of, the spiritual soul substance; image denotes a process that is primarily a physiological process in the brain, with occasional attempts to connect it with the soul in some fashion that would bridge the gap between mind and body. If in Spinoza the doctrine of the duality of existence is really at the bottom of the distinction between the attributes of thought and extension,—that is, if Spinoza really starts from Cartesian results,—we should expect to find the Cartesian distinction between image and idea reproduced in Spinoza. It is our purpose, however, to disprove this. In Spinoza the distinction is totally unanalogous to the Cartesian. The establishment of this claim retroactively corroborates the more general thesis. The more divergent the principles upon which the distinctions are made in the two cases, the more indisputable will be the claim that the two systems diverge radically in ways that are fundamental.

For Spinoza, the image is purely a physiological process. It is a phenomenon of body, an event in the world of existence. That is, as the human being is an existent, and is a part of nature, the image is an occurrence of exactly the same general type as other happenings in the existential series. "The affections of the human body, of which the ideas represent external bodies as present to us, we will call the images of things, though they do not record the figures of things. When the mind contemplates bodies in this fashion, we say that it imagines."[1] "The mind imagines any given body, because the human body is affected and disposed by the marks (*vestiguum*) of an external body, in the same manner as it is affected when certain of its parts are set in motion by the said external body."[2] Imagery is the representation of the empirical manifold of actuality, and the imagination is the organ of that representation. Images are bracketed with chimeras (whose nature is said to contain a manifest contradiction) and creatures of fancy, as not being realities at all.[3] We represent things by means of the imagination, which is connected with brain-processes,[4] and brain-processes Spinoza thinks of in the customary phraseology

[1] *Ethics*, Pt. 2, 17, note.
[2] *Ethics*, Pt. 2, 16.
[3] *Cogitata Metaphysica*, Vol. 4, Pt. I, ch. I.
[4] *ibid*, pp. 188–189.

of his day as movements of the animal spirits. Imagination, as we have already seen,[5] is a natural process serving as an instrument in assisting the mind in the attainment of conceptions.

Even in the *Cogitata Metaphysica*, as has been pointed out, Spinoza apparently does not use thinking substance as equivalent to immaterial substance, and, in fact, the latter term seems not to be used. He asserts that the notion of three souls, that of plants, of animals, and of man is an imaginary conception, for in matter there is nothing but mechanical forms and activities.[6] It is noteworthy that Spinoza offers as the reason why the conception of three souls is imaginary the fact of the mechanical nature of matter. Furthermore, in the same connection he attributes life only to those beings that have a soul united with a body, which means that life is to be attributed to men, and perhaps to animals, but *not to minds* or God. Now the term here used for "soul" is *anima*;[8] one can not resist the conclusion that soul here means for Spinoza a vital principle, something within the system of mechanical figures and textures, and not something akin to the spiritual substance of Descartes. Spinoza institutes an interesting contrast between mind and soul (*mens* and *anima*) by attributing life to a thing possessing a soul, but denying that life can be attributed to minds. Life he defines as the power by which things persist in their existence, in order to accommodate the meaning of the term to popular usage which attributes life to corporeal things not united with minds and to minds separated from bodies.[7] The terms *animus* and *spiritus* do not appear to be used in the *Cogitata Metaphysica*, except that *spiritus* appears in the sense of "animal spirits."

These statements and uses of terms seem to imply that Spinoza is concerned with two conceptions: The first, that of the soul (*anima*), the meaning of which is close to the primitive signification of the word and is free from psychological and metaphysical meanings; the second, that of mind (*mens*), which throughout the *Cogitata Metaphysica* seems to be related to essence. Mind is a class-name for the collection of concepts or essences as subjective, as known and possessed by the human being; and also, perhaps, for the power or possibility of having such essences. The possession of these concepts is what is signified by having a mind. It stands for the "forms" which are manifested or generated in the human being. Finally, the contexts do not give evidence that either word intends significations based upon the duality of substance as defined by Descartes.

But now turn to the idea. "By idea, I mean the conception of the mind which is formed by the mind as a thinking thing."[8] To this

[5] See above, pp. 67–68.
[6] *Cogitata Metaphysica*, Vol. 4, Pt. 2, ch. 6.
[7] *ibid.*
[8] *Ethics*, Pt. 2, def. 3.

Spinoza adds the following explanation: "I say conception rather than perception, because the word perception seems to imply that the mind is passive in respect to the object; whereas conception seems to express an activity of the mind." By this Spinoza is affirming the logical meaning in which he is employing the term. He is distinguishing it from "idea" in the sense of "idea of perception," that is, ideas as passively impressed upon the mind, coming in from the outside, or received in sense-perception. The conception expresses a logical function of the mind. The matter might be stated as follows: the question of the origin or derivation of ideas or knowledge, the question of how the mind comes to be furnished with its ideas, in the Lockian sense, is either subordinate, or else entirely absent, from Spinoza's thought, at least in this connection. He is rather concerned with the logical worth of the conception. This is borne out by the definition immediately following, that of the adequate idea. The idea is adequate when, considered in itself, "without relation to the object," it "has all the properties or intrinsic marks of a true idea." The explanation appended declares that "intrinsic" is used "in order to exclude that mark which is extrinsic, namely, the agreement of the idea with its object (*ideatum*)." That is, the test of the adequacy of the idea is in the idea itself, to be found in its coherence with other elements in a system of conceptions, and not in a correspondence to an ideate. He distinguishes ideas from images in the statement: "For by ideas, I do not understand images such as are formed in the bottom of the eye, or in the midst of the brain, but the conceptions of thought." [9] Despite this assertion, Spinoza does occasionally use "idea" as equivalent to image, or at least as referring to a physiological process. Idea, in the *De Emendatione*, is even said to be "in itself nothing else than a certain sensation," [10] and Spinoza's account of sensation is certainly free from all implications of the "psychical." Here as in some other places the idea is given a physiological interpretation; in short, it stands on the same level as the image.

But we now seem in danger of losing the distinction between image and idea which was taken as a characteristic doctrine. But the danger is only apparent, not real. The point is that the *psychological* account of idea and of thinking, in so far as Spinoza furnishes such an account, is of just the same nature as his account of image. It is a physiological process. As psychological fact, image and idea do not seem to differ at all. But the difference between them is derived from consideration of their cognitive function, their value in knowledge. From this view-point, the "idea" must be considered apart from all questions of its psychological nature. It means concept, but concept

9 *ibid*, p. 48, note.
10 Vol. I, p. 24.

not as a psychical entity, but as logical essence. It is a logical entity, not a psychological entity. The idea as concept is not an existent of any sort. According to Pollock, definition for Spinoza was almost what now-a-days would be called scientific explanation. It is "an equation of ideas corresponding to a constant relation between facts, and expressing the reduction of something unknown to terms of known elements." [11] If definition is the essence explicitly formulated, then surely by idea Spinoza meant something more akin to the scholastic form than an entity or state of immaterial soul substance.

It is the failure to recognize that the distinction between image and idea is of this nature that apparently is responsible for the opinion of Toennies (whose studies of Spinoza seem to be biassed by the errors of which so much has been said), that Propositions 5 et seq., of Part 2 of the *Ethics* are in contradiction with Axiom 3 of the same book. He says of these propositions that "in unserer Sprache zu reden, unter dem Namen Ding *jede* physische, unter dem Namen Idee *jede* psychische Erscheinung begriffen werden soll. Hiermit steht freilich schon das *dritte Axiom* desselben zweiten Theiles in Widerspruch. Hier werden *die Affecte* als besondere modi cogitandi von den Ideen unterschieden und diese deutlich genug als Arten der *Erkenntniss* aufgefasst; welche Auffassung freilich festgehalten wird, aber so, dass jene anderen Thatsachen des psychischen Lebens zunächst gänzlich vergessen werden" [12]. Toennies seems to understand Spinoza as meaning in the axiom that affections like love and desire, as well as ideas, are psychical states; and then takes the dictum (Prop. 7) that "the order and connection of ideas is the same as the order and connection of things" as standing for the parallelism of a psychical series to a material series. Taken so, it follows that Spinoza, in this statement of the parallelism, drops out of consideration all the elements of the psychical life save the ideas. To make up for this oversight, apparently, it would be necessary to revise Spinoza's dictum to read: "the order of ideas, affections, *etc.*, is the same as the order and connection of things"—which, as will appear later, would make nonsense of Spinoza's words. But if we recognize that by idea in the axiom and the propositions referred to Spinoza does not mean *psychological* (much less *psychical*) facts at all, but logical essences, no such difficulty appears.

We need not be content with this presumptuous emendation of Spinoza's dictum in refuting Toennies. We have, moreover, grounds for maintaining that the dictum contains only the term "idea," for the reason that affections are processes in the region of things, of extension, of nature. They are as much physical events as the rising of the sun.

[11] Pollock, *Spinoza, His Life and Times*, p. 147.

[12] Studien zur Entwicklungsgeschichte des Spinoza. *Vierteljahresschrift für wissenschaftliche Philosophie*, Vol. 7, p. 159.

And as events, they have their correlated ideas or logical essences. So that the dictum as it stands, instead of being deficient or inconsistent, precisely embodies Spinoza's meaning. The order and connection of things, of existents, including therein affections and emotions, correspond to the order and connection of ideas. The point is forcefully corroborated by the opening sentences of Part 3 of the *Ethics:* "Most writers on the emotions and on the nature of human life seem to be treating rather of things outside nature than of things following nature's general laws. They appear to conceive man to be situated in nature as a kingdom within a kingdom: for they believe that he disturbs rather than follows nature's order." And later he adds: "Nature's laws and ordinances, according to which all things are and change from one form to another, are everywhere and always the same; so that there should be one and the same method of understanding the nature of all things whatsoever, namely, through nature's universal laws and rules. Thus the passions of hatred, anger, envy, and so on, considered in themselves, follow from this same necessity and power of nature; in like manner they answer to certain definite causes, through which they are understood, and possess certain properties as worthy of being known as the properties of anything else." These sentences, serving as preface to a treatise on the emotions, are unmistakable in meaning, unless we vitiate the meaning of the passage by making "nature" signify the duality of existence. Without importing this foreign element, it is clear that affections are processes in existence, which have in the world of knowledge (not the world of the psychical) their correlated logical processes. The entire note to Proposition 2 of this Part indicates that Spinoza advances a mechanical conception of body and its states. "A mental decision and an appetite or determination of the body are simultaneous, or rather are one and the same thing, which we call decision, when it is regarded under and explained through the attribute of thought, and a determination, when it is regarded under the attribute of extension, and deduced from the laws of motion and rest." Clearly we are dealing with one thing here, not two assigned to different worlds.

Emotions are definitely ascribed to the body by their description as modifications of the body. "By EMOTION I mean the modifications of the body, whereby the power of acting of the body itself is increased or diminished, aided or constrained, and also the ideas of such modifications." [13] Emotion is also called a passivity of the soul, or confused idea. [14] The meaning of these phrases, and, in general, the reason why emotions are "ideas of the modifications of the body" are given in the following statement: "Now the power of the mind is defined by knowl-

---

[13] *Ethics*, Pt. 3, def. 3.
[14] *Ethics*, Pt. 3, "General Definition of the Emotions."

edge only, and its impotence or passion is defined by the privation of knowledge only."[15] To speak of emotions as confused or inadequate idea is to use an expression of logical, or cognitive, rather than psychological, import. Emotions "involve some clear and distinct conception," but the conception suffers from the obscuration characteristic of all confused and inadequate ideas.[16] And finally, it is worth nothing that the dictum of correspondence is formulated with especial reference to affectional states. "Even as thoughts and the ideas of things are ordered and associated in the mind, so are the modifications of the body or the images of things exactly in the same way ordered and associated in the body."[17] And Spinoza does not say "order and connection of ideas, emotions, affections."

The thesis of this essay receives a more or less indirect confirmation from Spinoza's polemic against the general idea or notion. His account of the general notion demonstrates clearly that the "idea" in his terminology can not be identified with the general notion or abstract idea. These notions, he says, are due to the inability of the imagination to form distinctly more than a certain number of images at a time. When the imagination is overburdened with images, it "imagines all bodies confusedly without any distinction;"[18] and this is the origin of the general or abstract idea. Such notions are extremely confused and vary greatly from individual; they are adventitious, variable, dependent upon the chance variations in the experience of individual men. Evidently the infinite mode of thought or series of ideas is not an aggregation of these empirically derived, confused, variable notions, nor a collection of individual streams of such notions. They are but confused images, and it "is not to be wondered at, that among philosophers, who seek to explain natural things merely by the images formed of them, so many controversies should have arisen."[19] The idea or pure concept is then a logical entity, wholly different in significance from the abstract ideas whose psychology has just been outlined.

This leads us to Spinoza's distinction between an association of ideas, which is the principle of memory, and a second association of ideas, which arises from the order of the intellect. A comparison of the two kinds of associations illustrates both the physiological character of the Spinozistic psychology and the purely logical character of the "idea." Memory is "nothing else than a certain association (*concatenatio*) of ideas involving the nature of things outside the human body, which association follows in the mind according to the order

[15] *Ethics*, Pt. 5, prop. 20, note.
[16] *Ethics*, Pt. 5, prop. 4, corol.
[17] *ibid*, prop. 1.
[18] *Ethics*, Pt. 2, prop. 40, note 1.
[19] *ibid*.

and association of the modifications (*affectiones*) of the human body. I say, first, it is an association of those ideas *only* (*tantum*), which involve the nature of things outside the human body; not of ideas which answer to (*explicant*) the nature of the said things: ideas of the modifications of the human body are, in truth, those which involve the nature both of the human body and of external bodies. I say, secondly, that this association follows according to the order and association of the modifications of the human body, in order to distinguish it from the association of ideas, which follows according to the order of the intellect, whereby the mind perceives things through their primary causes, and which is in all men the same." [20] One kind of ideas, involving the nature of outside things, is associated according to the order and connection of bodily modifications; this is memory, the order and association being evidently conceived in what we should call physiological terms. Compare the statement in which imagination is said to be "the idea by means of which the mind contemplates a thing as present; yet this idea indicates rather the present constitution of the human body than the nature of the external thing." [21] This sort of association of ideas is that which corresponds to inadequate knowledge, confused ideas—"hearsay," "mere experience," and perhaps is responsible for, or represents, inadequate inference. The ideas thus associated depend upon both the human body and outside things; this seems to mean simply that the physiological process is a function of two things, stimulus and bodily conditions. Now this set of ideas and manner of ordering ideas are in sharp contrast with ideas which *answer to*, or *explain*, the *nature* of the things outside, and this association arises from the order of the intellect. Here we are no longer in the domain of psychology, but of knowledge. These ideas, which, perhaps as psychological phenomena, would probably receive a physiological explanation similar to that given the other set, are cognitively the logical essences of things, and their connection is ideal and logical. The contrast is thus stated between connections of fact and connections of a logical nature. The use of the term "idea" in both instances is not a matter of terminological inconsistency, or a sign of a parallelistic hypothesis in the mind of the writer, unless we do violence to its intention by forcing such extraneous considerations upon the passage.

A search for an unmistakable enunciation of the theory of existence as dual, or of the principle of psychophysical parallelism, or finally of the spiritual status of the idea, would naturally lead to the work in which Spinoza is commenting on the philosophy of Descartes. But even in the *Cogitata Metaphysica* where, if anywhere, we should expect

[20] *Ethics*, Pt. 2, p. 18, note (italics mine).
[21] *Ethics*, Pt. 5, p. 34.

to find prominent the duality of existence and its resultant psychological conceptions, Spinoza's teaching is fairly free from opportunities for misconstructions in terms of a spiritualistic psychology. Other things being equal, Spinoza is in accord with Hobbes. The ensuing quotations are as illuminating as any that could be selected. "Finally, entity of the mind (*ens rationis*) is nothing more than a mode of thinking, which renders easier the retaining, explaining, and imagining of known things. Herewith is to be noted, that by mode of thinking we understand . . . all affections of thought, such as understanding (*intellectus*), joy, imagination, *etc.*" [22] This statement assigns understanding and emotion to the same level as memory and imagination. Now we find shortly after that "imagination is indeed nothing else than to feel those traces which appear in the cerebrum because of the motion of the spirits which are excited in the senses by objects." [23] It is evident that Spinoza has in mind the common notion of animal spirits, and that this is the leading idea in his physiological psychology. And furthermore, so far as these statements go, understanding is as much a physiological process as memory, imagination, and emotion.

Let us recall at this point Spinoza's distinction between *ens rationis*, *modus cogitandi*, and *idea*. The first is described as a mode of thinking, and we have seen that joy and understanding are cited as such modes. Now the modes of thinking are not *ideas*, for only the idea has an ideate which necessarily exists or can exist. But Spinoza asserts emphatically that the division of being into *ens reale* and *ens rationis* is illegitimate and a source of error among the "verbal philosophers." The true division is between being whose essence necessarily involves existence and that which involves existence only in possibility, but not necessarily. This division, however, does not parallel the division into real entities and entities of the mind. We can not say that real entity corresponds to entity which necessarily exists and that entity of the mind corresponds to entity which may, but does not necessarily, exist. Let us, therefore, put aside, following Spinoza's own injunction, the division into *ens reale* and *ens rationis*. There remains, however, something that Spinoza thinks can correctly be termed *ens rationis*— what is it? We learn that if we mean by the words the modes of thinking, they are real entities; but as real entities they are not ideas, are neither true nor false, but can only be called, like love, good or bad. On the other hand, if we signify by the phrase something other than the modes of thinking, it is pure nothingness. That is, what we should call "mental entity" is pure nothingness; there is no such kind of entity or existence. By "mental entity" we must mean either an idea,

[22] *Cogitata Metaphysica*, Vol. 4, Pt. I, ch. I
[23] *ibid.*

that is, an essence, a pure logical function, or else we must mean thinking processes themselves. The first use of these words Spinoza de-
plores, for he specifically states that mental entities are not ideas.
But granting the first usage, as idea, nothing psychological, much less
anything spiritual or psychical, is intended. In the second, a usage
which Spinoza seems inclined to admit, as thinking process, we have
something which is a natural process in existence and has just been so
described.

But what then is fictitious entity? It is not to be confounded (as
many do confound it) with the *ens rationis*, asserting that it "has no
existence outside of the mind;" for this assertion presupposes precisely
that distinction between *ens rationis* and *ens reale* which has just been
discarded as invalid. Finally, the *ens fictum* is not a mode of thinking
like imagination or understanding. It is simply a union of terms
(*terminus*) effected in an arbitrary manner by the will alone without any
reason for so doing. The *ens rationis*, on the contrary, depends
neither on the will, nor consists of a uniting of different terms. Spinoza's thought in these difficult passages [24] may be summarized as follows: modes of thinking such as imagination are real entities, for they
are processes in nature; they are not ideas, but as real entities have
their corresponding essences or concepts, their definitions and "scientific" causal explanations. Fictions, from the standpoint of knowledge,
are unclear and indistinct ideas, and are worthless cognitively; but
as "psychological" facts they are arbitrary combinations of the presentations of imagination and sense,—facts, therefore, of nature and
human nature. Logically and cognitively they are not knowledge
and do not represent anything. As facts, with reference to their
causes, they are products of will and imagination. With reference
to knowledge, the chimera differs from the fiction, for the former
involves a manifest contradiction and can not possibly be true; the
latter is rather characterized by unclearness and indistinctness, and
*may* be true. But as psychological facts, chimera and fictions are on
the same basis. As we have seen, they are brain-processes, for imagination is the operation of the animal spirits in the cerebrum. The
true point at issue in this whole discussion is, as Spinoza indicates,
the confining of the meaning of entity of the mind to modes of thinking,
and the rejection of any other meaning, together with the whole
scheme of thought represented by the division of entities into real and
mental.

Spinoza then proceeds to carry out his division of being. The
being of essence (*esse essentiae*) is being whose essence involves existence; it is "nothing else than that mode under which created things
are comprehended in the attributes of God." Being of idea (*esse*

[24] *cf. Cogitata Metaphysica*, Vol. 4, ch. 1, pp. 189–190.

*ideae*) is being in so far as everything is contained objectively (*objective*) in the idea of God. Being of possibility (*esse potentiae*) refers to the power of God, by which He could create all things not yet existing from his absolute liberty of will. Being of existence (*esse existentiae*) is the essence itself of things considered as outside God and in themselves, and is apportioned to things after they have been created by God.[25] These kinds of being, including the *esse potentiae*, are separated only in things, but in no wise in God. Now what we have called the system of logical essences or concepts, the body of truth, which forms the thought attribute is evidently what Spinoza intends by *esse ideae*. The term "objective" in Spinoza has a meaning almost the inverse of what the term now means. But if we put "subjective" in its place in the definition of *esse ideae*, it must be noted that *esse ideae* refers to everything as contained in the *idea of God*, not as contained in, or dependent on, a knowing finite mind. The supplanting of one term by the other does not make, and should not be allowed to make, the *esse ideae* a matter of the knowing subject, knowing consciousness, or psychical knowing soul. The "subject" implied is the idea of God. So that *esse ideae* means everything in so far as the "ideas" or concepts of things depend upon, or are contained in, the idea of God. The *esse essentiae* looked upon as the body of rational truth or knowledge, but aside from all question as to the particular knowing subject, is the *esse ideae*. Being of idea of a thing, therefore, stands for the logical essence of the thing taken in its systematic and logical relation to the idea, or thought essence, of God. The parallelism of the modes of the attributes as knowledge or truth is a parallelism of logical essences (*esse ideae*) to the system of things, the existential series, that is, *esse existentiae*. Basically the distinction is one between form (essence) and matter (existence, actuality), as Spinoza himself indicates.[26] From this summary it appears, consequently, that by "idea" Spinoza has no thought of signifying some entity of a psychological nature, and still less to denote a psychical fact of any sort. The division of being is logical, not psychological. His explicit rejection of the notion of mental entity, save in the one sense of a mode of thinking such as understanding and imagination, which are natural phenomena like sunset or sunrise, evinces his impatience with distinctions between existences based on psychological considerations.

Having examined the *Cogitata Metaphysica* with a view to discovering grounds for credence in Spinoza's putative inclination towards psychophysical parallelism or the Cartesian dual view of existence, let us next consider the *Short Treatise*. A translator of this work finds in it the "first formulation of the Law of Parallelism which plays

[25] *cf. Cogitata Metaphysica*, Pt. I, ch. 2.
[26] *Cogitata Metaphysica*, Vol. 4, Pt. I, ch. 2, last paragraph.

such a prominent part in the psychology of to-day."[27] If this can be substantiated, doubt is thrown upon the thesis of this essay. On the contrary, however, it is not difficult to demonstrate that this "discovery" is a good example of the common fallacy in Spinozistic exegesis. A brief survey of the discussion of soul and body, idea and understanding, given in the treatise is sufficient to vindicate this claim.

In its general theses, the *Short Treatise* is not at variance with the three other works that have been considered. Essence and existence are its dominating concepts. In minor points there are differences. Thus the distinction between *entia rationis* and *entia realia* is apparently accepted. The former seems to comprise elements, such as images, not included under the term in what was regarded as a possible legitimate use in the *Cogitata Metaphysica*. For "some things being in our understanding and not in Nature, and so these alone being also only our own work, they serve to understand things distinctly; among them we comprehend all relations which have reference to several objects; and these we call *Entia Rationis*."[28] But Spinoza evidently does not mean by *entia rationis* anything inconsistent with the psychological view-point that has been described.

Truth reveals itself.[29] The highest type of thought is a rational intuitive comprehension that has no need of discursive thinking.[30] Understanding is a name we give to "all the ideas which every one has," and of which we "make a whole."[31] By idea Spinoza means essence. He distinguishes between ideas which arise necessarily from the reality of things, together with the essence in God, and the ideas which exhibit to us the things now existing by their effects on us. This distinction is made in connection with the statement that, "Between the Idea and the object there must necessarily be a union, since the one can not be without the other; for there is no thing the idea of which is not in the thinking thing and no idea can be unless the thing also exists."[32] This statement refers only to the first of the two kinds of ideas enumerated. The reason is clear, for we can have ideas of things, that is, images, without the thing itself existing. Understanding is consequently a name for the collection of essences—the whole of ideas which every one has.

Now the crucial question is this: are Spinoza's remarks concerning body and soul capable of being construed as an expression of a dualistic view, in such a sense that a contrast of spiritual and physical aspects of existence, or a statement of the Law of Parallelism, is implied? It must be admitted that he constantly conjoins the terms

---

[27] *God, Man, and Human Welfare*, Open Court Publishing Co., 1909, Translator's note, p. 120.
[28] *Korte Verhandeling*, Vol. 4, p. 35.
[29] *ibid*, p. 61.
[30] *ibid*, p. 39.
[31] *ibid*, p. 19.
[32] *ibid*, p. 78, note.

"body" and "soul," and the terms indicate some sort of distinction or difference of point of view. The question is, *what* sort? And does the distinction amount to a dualism, or is it largely a matter of verbal convenience?

What has Spinoza to say about the soul? "This knowledge, *idea, etc.*, of each particular thing which actually comes to be is, we say, the soul (*ziel*) of this particular thing."[33] But every particular thing is a certain proportion of motion and rest, we are told, and these we call bodies; the difference between bodies is the difference between their respective proportions of motion and rest.[34] "Out of these proportions of motion and rest comes also actually to be this body of ours; of which, then, not less than of all other things, knowledge, an Idea, *etc.*, must be in the thinking thing, and, therefore, our soul also."[35] The idea of the body, of *any* body, is the soul of that body. Does the statement imply anything more than that every existing thing has an essence or idea which it embodies, or actualizes, and that what we are pleased to call "our soul" is simply the essence, knowledge, or idea, (the form?), of what we are pleased to call "our body?" So far nothing unique is attributed to "our body;" it is not exceptional in possessing a soul—everything, as Spinoza says, has a soul. A triangle, for example, has a soul, namely, the concept or logical entity which is its truth. And furthermore, the soul-ideas of various bodies seem to be on the same level.

As the body changes continually, so does its idea or cognition in the thinking thing.[36] But this can hardly be twisted into an assertion that for every bodily change there is a corresponding "mental" or "psychical" change, that there is a parallelism of two different and contrasted series. For that would make nonsense of what has just been written by Spinoza. Perhaps Spinoza's real meaning can be clarified by an analogy. Suppose we draw a curve, say a parabola; corresponding to the moments of the curve are the moments of its equation as it is explicated, but the changes in the curve follow a law, are within limits. So as the body changes, "ours" or any other, so does its "equation," its soul. But the changes are within limits, for if the proportion of motion and rest passes certain bounds, the result is death.[37] When we are aware of the changes in "our body," we have feeling.[38]

It would require some ingenuity to read out of these statements real support for the contention that Spinoza is writing about the Law of Parallelism. It is not difficult, however, to see that he is concerned

[33] *ibid*, p. 37, note 6.
[34] *ibid*, p. 37, notes 7 and 8.
[35] *ibid*, p. 37, note 9.
[36] *ibid*, p. 37, note 10.
[37] *ibid*, p. 37, note 14.
[38] *ibid*, p. 37, note 13.

with the correlation of the logical essence or truth of a thing with the thing as existent. And it must be contended that this correlation can not be identified with the parallelism between spiritual soul-state and the physical body-process.

Question may arise, however, concerning the thinking thing in which the idea-souls of things are said to be. Now the thinking thing can not be the "soul" (however we may wish to define it). For, first, all existing things have souls; and secondly, the soul, since it is the idea of the thing, is the very entity that is said to be in the thinking thing. This thinking thing appears to be the thought attribute, and in final analysis, God or Substance. No attribute is in man which was not first to be found in nature; as a mode of the attributes of God, his soul, or idea, or cognition (to use terms as juxtaposed by Spinoza) is in God, the thinking thing, which is to say, God as essence, as truth.[39] All that man possesses of thought are modes of the thinking attribute ascribed to God.[40] In this lies the eternity of the soul.

So far our citations have been statements, metaphysical in meaning, affording little latitude for psychological interpretation. We can now turn to those statements which seem more susceptible to interpretations at variance with the thesis of this essay.

In a note on the Will [41] Spinoza refers to a union of body and soul such as is commonly assumed by philosophers. But he does not inform us what sort of a union that is. Further, he refers to it only for the sake of argument. Conceivably this may mean that he has in mind the Cartesian type of body-soul union, but this, however, can be only a conjecture, since he himself says nothing more of it.

It is in the chapter "Our Blessedness," where the problem of moral control, freedom from the passions, and evil are of primary interest, that the statements occur which are most susceptible to the "parallelistic" version. "The chief effect of the other attribute (the thinking attribute) is an idea (*Begrip*) of things so that when it (the thinking attribute?) comes to conceive them, either love or hate, *etc.*, will arise therefrom. This effect, then, since it does not bring extension with it, can not be ascribed to extension, but only to the thinking (attribute); so that the cause of all the changes, which arise in this mode, must be sought, not in extension, but only in the thinking thing." [42] In the translation of the *Short Treatise* referred to above, this passage is translated as follows: "The most important effect of the other attribute (thought) is such a comprehension of things that after the soul conceives them, either love, hate, or some other passion will arise. Since this effect does not involve extension, it (the effect) can not be

[39] *ibid*, p. 79, note.
[40] *ibid*, p. 37.
[41] *ibid*, p. 63, note 2.
[42] *ibid*, p. 73.

ascribed to that extension, but only to thought, so that the cause of all the changes which occur in this mode (the mode of thought) must by no means be sought in extension, but only in the thinking thing." [43] In a note appended to this remark, the translator asserts that the statement is "the first formulation of the Law of Parallelism which plays such a prominent part in the psychology of to-day." Before commenting upon this, it is advisable to place Spinoza's words in their context.

In the immediately preceding paragraphs, Spinoza is interested in showing that in extension there is nothing but motion and rest, and that only through motion and rest can motion and rest be changed. It follows that "no mode of thinking in the body can bring about either motion or rest." [44] Then he proceeds to point out that the direction of the motion of a body may change, just as I might stretch out my arm, and thereby bring to pass that the spirits (*geesten*) which had their motion in one direction change it to another direction, according to the "form of the spirits." "The cause of this is . . . that the soul (*ziel*), being an Idea of the body, is united with the same in such a manner that it and the body taken together form one whole." Now the term *geest* Spinoza uses in the plural. In the translation just referred to, the following note is appended to the term "spirits" by which *geesten* is rendered: "Schaarschmidt inserts *Lebens* in parenthesis, '(Lebens) Geister', *i.e.*, life-spirits. It is obvious here that Spinoza means by this concrete figure the spiritual aspect of existence which in other places he calls 'thought' or 'consciousness'" (p. 119). The reader is referred back to this note in the next chapter where the term is again used in the plural. [45]

But is it credible that these passages contain a formulation of the Law of Parallelism or that Spinoza intends by "spirits" the spiritual aspect of existence, or consciousness? In the first place, he has just denied that anything but motion and rest can effect a change in extension. So if *geesten* means anything akin to the psychical, or spirit in the sense defined by the old dualism, that is, something of a nature opposed to extension, the later statement that the spirits can change the direction of motion is in contradiction with the earlier statement. In objection to this accusation of contradiction, the following defense may be offered: it may be said that in the later passage Spinoza asserts merely that the spirits can change the direction, but not the amount, of motion, so that there is no contradiction. But this seems to be a devious and laborious method of avoiding the obvious signification of the term *geesten* in favor of ideas imported into Spinoza's

---

[43] *God, Man, and Human Welfare*, p. 120.

[44] Vol. 4, p. 73.

[45] *God, Man, and Human Welfare*, p. 129, translator's note. *cf.* Spinoza's note, Van V. and L., Vol. 4, p. 77, pp. 82–83.

thought. Schaarschmidt's emendation is obviously correct. Here as elsewhere Spinoza is utilizing the familiar conception of "animal spirits." [46]  Only by a violent distortion can these statements be regarded as having anything to do with parallelism.

We have then four terms: soul, spirits, idea of the body (as soul of the body), and body.  Now if Spinoza is not writing in terms of the parallelism of psychical mode to physical mode, one might fairly ask, what sort of distinction does he draw between soul, spirits, idea, and body?  The soul (*ziel*) is spoken of as changing the direction of the movements of the spirits (p. 74); and influence of body on soul and of soul on body is considered (p. 74).  That the soul and the body have no relation (community, *gemeenschap*) with each other is also claimed (p. 78).  All these remarks need explication.

Now in connection with these statements and in defense of our position a general observation is apposite; namely, that a distinction between body and soul does not necessarily mean a distinction of the type defined by a dualism of substances.  We need not assume that every one after Descartes who uses the terms "soul" or "spirit" or "thought" has Descartes's spiritual substance in mind.

The uncertainties that attach to Spinoza's discussions of the soul in the *Short Treatise* originate in the fact that the term is employed in several senses.  The various significations of the term are not all specifically defined, but they can be discriminated.  First, by "soul" is meant the essence or idea of an existent.  In this sense a soul is defined as the idea or cognition of a body.  Secondly, "soul" is on occasion equivalent to thinking power or faculty; it is a name denoting the concrete psychological fact that thinking goes on, a name for an activity of the organism; to have a soul (in this employment of the word) is almost equivalent to the vernacular expression, "to have brains."  Thirdly, soul seems to stand for a vital principle governing the functions of the body, the source of its energies.  In the second and third senses the term is applicable only to animate beings, perhaps only to human beings.  But in the first meaning it applies to every existent without exception.

Correspondingly there are three ways of drawing a distinction between soul and body.  First, soul and body are distinguished as essence from existence, as form from matter, as mode from mode, but not as substance from substance.  In these terms, soul and body may be said to have nothing in common, for they are as diverse as the thinking and extended attributes.  The differentiation is metaphysical.

Secondly, soul and body are separated as power or function or capacity from that which possesses this capacity or that in which this function resides.  Soul in this signification of the word, however, is a

<hr />

[46] *cf. Ethics*, Pt. 2, prop. 17.

going-on in existence—it is in the world of extension, so to speak. This differentiation is psychological. The fact of thinking is, therefore, causally to be explained in terms of the physiological conception most available at that time, namely, the notion of "animal spirits." To state that the soul directs the flow of the animal spirits would no more imply the spirituality of the soul than the statement that the brain exercises a control over the flow of nerve-currents would imply the spirituality of the brain.

Thirdly, a distinction between soul as vital principle and the body as its instrument. Soul is to be thought of as a sort of active principle informing the body, guiding the operations of the animal spirits. But here soul is as physiological as body.

Now it is the oscillations between these various meanings that are largely responsible for the apparent inconsistencies to be found in the *Short Treatise*, particularly in Chapters 19 and 20 of Part 2. Spinoza's problem inevitably requires such changes in the employment of the term. For he is interested in establishing his deepest conviction that clear and distinct ideas, true knowledge, will enable us to control the passions. He is obliged, consequently, to relate the soul, on the one hand, to knowledge of essence; while, on the other hand, it must be connected with the organism, as an informing, controlling principle that can be affected by the body and can in turn affect it. For knowledge is knowledge of essence; and passions are bodily changes. The metaphysical point of view shifts to the psychological or physiological, and the latter is forsaken in turn for the metaphysical. The transition is through the fact of cognition. For the passions are connected with opinion (p. 71, note), and human welfare, which signifies release from the passions, is secured only by the highest form of knowledge. Such knowledge involves a penetration by the soul as cognitive intuitive power of the infinite realm of essence so that man may be identified with God, with Substance, with completed reality. We must know God, and then we shall be united with him. We need not know him completely, for a partial knowledge of him will lead to that union with him which is our blessedness and is knowledge of "the most excellent things." Spinoza points out that we do not know fully our own body, yet we are intimately united with it and have great love for it (p. 81). The real issue is thus clarified: how are we to attain to such a knowledge of God as will effect the transfer of our love for our body, that is, for the contingent and the transient, to God, to the Universal and the Eternal? The union can be brought about only through knowledge of essence, and the knowledge of essence must in some fashion exert a control over the passions. It is this problem which necessitates Spinoza's shifting from the metaphysical and epistemological world of discourse to that of psychology and physiology.[47]  Only on some such basis as this can we appreciate that the seemingly glaring inconsistencies in Spinoza's language are apparent, not genuine.

There are certain conclusions that this discussion discloses.  The chief is this: in no case does the differentiation of "body" from "soul" force upon us the belief that Spinoza intends to set over against a corporeal, extended, material body an incorporeal, psychical, or spiritual soul.  Soul does not mean consciousness as a series of psychical mental states or spiritual entities in opposition to a series of physical events, or the spiritual, as opposed to the physical, aspect of existence.

As a final corroboration of the thesis, let us turn to the *Appendix* of the treatise, where Spinoza seeks to "express the essence of the soul."

First of all we learn that the soul has its origin in the body, that its changes depend alone upon the body, and in this consists the union of body and soul (p. 96).  Further "in extension there are no other modifications than motion and rest . . . the human body is nothing other than a certain proportion of motion and rest.  The objective essence, then, of which the real proportion is in the thinking attribute is, we say, the soul of the body; so whenever one of these two modifications changes to more or less (motion or rest) so is the idea too changed in a similar degree" (p. 99).  "Seeing that for the real existence of an idea (or objective essence) no other thing is required except the thinking attribute and the object (or formal essence), it is certain . . . that the idea, or objective essence, is the most immediate modification of the attribute.  In the thinking attribute, therefore, there can be given no other modification which can belong to the essence of the soul of a similar (every?) thing, than only the idea of such an actually existing thing, which must necessarily be in the thinking attribute: for such an idea brings with itself the other modifications, Love, Desire, *etc.*" (pp. 96–97).  "If we should go on to ascribe to the essence of the soul that by means of which alone it can really exist, we would be able to find nothing other than the attribute and the object of which we have just spoken; and neither of these can belong to the essence of the soul, since the object has nothing of Thinking and is distinguished actually from the soul . . . Therefore, then, the essence of the soul consists alone in this, namely, in the being of an Idea or objective essence in the thinking attribute, arising from the essence of an object, which indeed actually exists in Nature.  I say *of an object which actually exists* without more particularity, in order to comprehend herein not only the modifications of extension, but also the modifications of all the infinite attributes, which likewise have a soul, as well as extension" (p. 97).

Certainly this account can be regarded as dealing with spiritual

[47] *cf.* ch. 22.

existence, or aspect of existence, only by doing violence to its spirit and direct expression. The idea is represented as the formal essence, a logical thought entity. Existence is confined to extension, or to extension and attributes other than the attribute of thought. The essence of the soul is just its being an idea in the thinking attribute. The idea-object correlation is the correspondence of the essence with the existent: and this correlation is the relation of soul and body, in the metaphysical and epistemological sense.

The end of thinking is to bring forth "an infinite Idea, which comprehends objectively (*voorwerpelijk*) in itself the whole of Nature, such as it actually is in itself" (p. 96). The possession of this infinite idea is the highest estate of the soul—or rather, it *is* the soul in its subsumption under the attribute of thought, the soul as united with God. It is at this point of our discussion that we can comprehend Spinoza's "thinking being" and its relation to the soul. The thinking being in nature is a single thing, "which is expressed in infinite Ideas, according to the infinite things which are in Nature" (p. 79). This single thinking thing is the attribute of thought, it is God as thought. If we apply to essence the distinction between *natura naturans* and *natura naturata*, the essences present themselves in twofold guise. On the one hand, God as thought or essence, corresponding to *natura naturans;* on the other hand, the infinite number of essences, the idea-souls of the infinite numbers of things, corresponding to *natura naturata*. The soul as essence is thus on the one hand an essence amid an infinite number of essences; on the other, it is in God, as Supreme Essence. The duty of thinking is to attain such a comprehension of essences that their unity is envisaged, that the soul can know itself as essence contained in the infinite essence. Since the idea which is the soul of a thing "can find no rest in the knowledge of the body without passing over to the knowledge of that without which the body and the idea itself can neither be nor be conceived, so the soul becomes immediately united by love to this latter" (p. 82). Thereby we are united in love with the "incorporeal subject," and this is our second birth, our regeneration (p. 82).

Finally, we are in a position to comment correctly upon Spinoza's use of the words "spirit" (*geest* used in the singular), and "incorporeal." The corporeal and the incorporeal, the flesh and the spirit, are contrasted (p. 83). Is this, then, a lapse into Cartesian dualistic modes of thought? The answer is that we are by no means compelled to assume this. These distinctions are primarily moral, as the context shows, not metaphysical. But the distinction between the corporeal and the incorporeal might be drawn by Spinoza as a metaphysical distinction without involving the dualistic view so often imputed to him. For the essences are incorporeal, like the medieval forms. The incorporeal subject is God as Essence or Truth. This means the ideality of essence and of God as Essence. To become attached to incorporeal things signifies that we apprehend and are in union with the perdurable essences and truths of things and are free from the trammels of the contingent and transient. The spiritual being of the soul for Spinoza means that the soul is in union with God, with the infinite and eternal, that it has attained the clearest vision of rational insight. It is the soul *sub quadam specie aeternitatis*. What man has of thought, that is what we are to denote by "soul." In the sphere in which Spinoza's mind is moving, the familiar dualisms between body and soul, spirit and matter, the psychical and the physical, conscious state and physiological process, the world of spiritual existence and the world of material existence, have no place, no relevancy. To interpret his doctrine on a basis of such dual conceptions obscures the genuine difficulties of his system beneath a cloud of problems alien to the world of his thought, and, therefore, in reference to his doctrine, extrinsic and artificial.

There is, however, one other point that might be appealed to in defense of the position that has been the object of attack. It is this: Spinoza repudiates the notion that mind sets body in motion and asserts that such statements are merely verbal and empty of meaning.[48] Now this may be by some called a repudiation of interactionism and, therefore, a tacit admission of the theory of the dual character of existence. From this, then, might be derived some indirect justification for the "parallelistic" interpretation of Spinoza. But this need not give us pause. For to Spinoza, construed as we have understood him, interaction of mind and body would not merely be as impossible as it would be were he the most stubborn of modern parallelists, but more, it would be senseless. Mind, as the thought attribute, or series of logical essences, or truth, could in no sense be looked upon as interacting with body; for it is impossible to understand how anything but an existent could interact with an existent. One might as well talk of the concept of a triangle interacting with the triangle drawn upon the blackboard. Besides, a denial that mind influences body cuts two ways: it may just as well depend on a disbelief in a substantial spiritual principle and an adherence to a psychology like that of Hobbes as on an advocacy of a two-substance theory. Spinoza's statement might legitimately, perhaps, be held as a rejection of Descartes's position that the mind could direct the flow of the animal spirits; and yet the rejection might be regarded as resulting from a negation of the doctrine of the dualism of existence rather than following from an acceptance of that doctrine.

It is worth pointing out that in the *Short Treatise*, as has been shown,

48 *cf. Ethics*, Pt. 3, p. 2, and note.

Spinoza does speak of the soul as changing the direction of the animal spirits. Is this then in contradiction with the statement from the *Ethics?* It need not be so taken. In the former work the term "soul" (*ziel*) is favored, if not exclusively used, in discussions of the influence of the soul on the body and of body on the soul. In the section of the *Ethics* just referred to, the term used is "mind" (*mens*). Now we have observed that "soul" is employed in more than one sense in the treatise. In one acceptation, it stands for idea or cognition; and in this sense it is what Spinoza elsewhere calls "mind." It was observed, further, that in other employments of the term there was no difficulty in understanding that the soul could direct the spirits. The soul as an activity of the organism, or as the vital principle, could be conceived as operating in this fashion without encountering any of the dualistic stumbling-blocks. There is, then, no necessity for taking the two works as contradictory. When the term is used in what was called the metaphysical and epistemological significations, which usage renders it equivalent to mind as the essences or thought attribute, we are outside the sphere of psychological and physiological considerations. In this case it is nonsense to ask whether the mind or soul sets body in motion. In the *Ethics*, in the section referred to, we are in the metaphysical and cognitive sphere, and the statement is compatible with the point of view of the *Treatise*.

On the customary basis of interpretation, Spinoza's statements that the soul of a thing is the idea of a thing, that soul is the idea of body, and that the idea of body is mind, are highly confusing. But these expressions are in accord with the interpretation presented in this essay—in fact, they are just the sort of expressions that would naturally follow from his general position and terminological usages.

We may conclude that Spinoza's psychology is in general like that of Hobbes, and that his treatment of the psychological problems involved in the notions of body, soul, image, emotion, and idea is not guided by influences supposed to emanate from the Cartesian dualism of substance. The distinction between image and idea is not a distinction that obtains within the psychological field, nor is it Cartesian. The latter is a distinction in existence; the Spinozistic is not even comparable thereto. Indeed, it might conduce to clearness not to speak of such a distinction at all. The real point is that ideas, images, sensations, perceptions, emotions, as psychological phenomena, are on the same footing, and fall within the same field; they are names for various activities of the human being, explicable by physiological principles. The preferred term for mental process seems to be image. But from the point of view of knowledge, the mental process (the term now referring to meaning and value) is an idea, a conception. In psychological treatment, the nature, origin, and conditions of the activity of thinking are in question: in connection with knowledge, it is the logical structure and implications of thought that are up for elucidation. Body and soul are distinguished in more than one way, but the distinctions can not be equated with the Cartesian distinction and show little or no sign that the Cartesian doctrine represents their source. And, finally, the thesis that Spinoza's parallelism of ideas and things is a correspondence of logical entities and actually existing things, and not a parallelism of mental or spiritual entities or conscious states with physical changes, seems to have been substantiated.


## V

In the light of the preceding discussion, it may be illuminating to examine the features of Spinoza's system when the assumption is made that his work rests upon and expresses the conception of psychophysical parallelism, with its allied conception of psychoneural parallelism. In a negative way further support for the thesis of this essay may be obtained. Let us, therefore, assume that Spinoza was a psychophysical parallelist, and that the attribute of thought denotes psychical or spiritual existence, and that the idea is a psychical entity. With this as the guiding conception, let us observe what difficulties and inconsistencies arise. That is, we shall take the position that the Cartesian doctrine of the duality of body and mind, and of substances in general, is the basis of Spinoza's work, assuming that as a logical consequence the latter is led to the "first formulation of the Law of Psychophysical Parallelism." It may then be possible to estimate the legitimacy of these assumptions by the degree of consistency and harmony within the body of Spinozistic teaching obtained by this method.

The transformation of Spinoza into the great exponent of psychophysical parallelism is a trick of many commentators because their accounts involve the assumption of the essential continuity of Cartesian and Spinozistic doctrines. Toennies [1] affords an illustration. Following the remarks already cited, he goes on to say that "Der Gedanke, welcher dort [2] und in folgenden Saetzen ausgefuehrt wird, laesst sich auf eine einfache Weise so wiedergeben: Jeder Partikel physischen (materiellen, koerperlichen) Daseins entspricht einem Partikel psychischen (immateriellen, geistigen) Daseins, welcher in Wirklichkeit (oder in Gott) mit ihr identisch, oder, was wiederum dasselbe sagt, das Bewusstsein von ihr ist. Wenn wir ein System von physischen Partikeln einen Koerper nennen und das entsprechende System von psychischen Partikeln einen Geist, so gehoert dieser Geist zu diesem Koerper, ist

[1] *Op. cit.*, pp. 159–160.
[2] Pt. 2, prop. 11.

seine Idee oder sein Bewusstsein."[3] Now we are contending that this misrepresents Spinoza's fundamental meaning. In order to clear up the matter, let us pursue the interpretation on a basis similar to this of Toennies. We shall then find perplexities whose artificiality suggests their origin in misinterpretation, and the irrelevance of that doctrine.

Construed in these terms, Spinoza's analysis of the psychological fact possesses the following features, reading from within outwards: (1) the conscious mental psychical state; (2) the physiological process correlated therewith; (3) the stimulating extra-organic object (the metaphysical mode of the attribute of extension). There is a one to one correlation of the mental order with the physical order. Now we may inquire: Is the image a psychical fact and, therefore, spiritual? If this be the case, how are we to account for the physiological explanation of the image? Do we find the image to be a hybrid thing, a composite of utterly dissimilar elements? Our scheme is incomplete if this interpretation of Spinoza's words is to be conscientiously followed out, for there must be a doubling of the psychical series. Since we have now made the distinction between idea and image a psychological one, the characteristic phrase, "ideas of images," must be given a place in the scheme. Therefore, we must find room in the psychical order for, (1) ideas, (2) image-parallels; and in the physical order for (1) physiological correlates of ideas and images, the difference between them being undetermined, and (2) external sources of stimulation. Or, finally, leaving the image as purely physiological, we have a correlation of three things—idea, physiological image, and external object. In the one case there is fourfold correspondence, in the other threefold.

Now if it is pointed out that such a situation is obviously artificial, the retort is that this is precisely what is to be indicated. It is clear that the more we insist upon foisting upon Spinoza the notion of existence as dual, and the incommensurability of the two orders of existence, the less simple becomes the status of the image. Peculiarities in the language of Spinoza heap new difficulties upon those encountered by Descartes.

If there be any need to illustrate further the puzzles that follow such a course of procedure, one might inquire what is to be done with Spinoza's *"idea ideae,"* and similar expressions. Without adding more, we may conclude that the strict application of the two realms of existence theory forces into consideration difficulties that are suspiciously artificial. It is impossible to believe that they are legitimate or represent Spinoza.

One more point remains to be considered. If Spinoza be taken as a thorough psychophysical parallelist, the parallelism of the modes

[3] *cf.* p. 170, and second article, p. 335.

tends to collapse through the elision of the order of extension, as has
been noted by more than one commentator. For if the idea is a psychical spiritual entity, the order of extension—the material world—
can exist for the knowing mind only as a set of spirit entities called
ideas-of-extension. The incommensurability of thought and extension,
their coordination without interdependence, encloses knowledge in the
sphere of ideas and certifies that all that is knowable is the mental
psychical order. If the element of thought be totally unlike the unit
in the world of extension, the correspondence of the one with the
other can not be given as a fact of experience. For experience is,
according to these principles, psychical or mental experience, and in
order to experience extension, extension must be mental, and, therefore, must be spiritualized. Which amounts to saying that in order
for extension to be a factor of experience, it must assume the form of
non-extended extension, for it must be psychical and spiritual. And
this is to land in utter contradiction. It literally amounts to the
assertion that the mind can not know or experience extension without
imperiling the existence of that extension. The frequent averring by
commentators that, in the last analysis, Spinoza's doctrine requires
only thought to exist is an inescapable conclusion, if our philosopher
was couching his thought in psychophysical terms. The field of the
physical is excluded from the field of actual experience and knowledge
since that experience and knowledge are and can be only spiritual,
and the existences experienced and known only psychical. Accordingly, to be, and to be conceived, to be actual and to be experienced,
and, finally, to be in the mind or soul, are only different ways of saying
to be in consciousness or to be psychical. For being, conception,
actuality, experience, if they are to mean anything, must stand for
differentiations in the series of psychical states.

Had this subjectivistic construction of his thought been the final
goal of Spinoza's philosophy, we might properly expect him to give
some explicit recognition of the fact. Or at least we might look for
him to take some notice of the resultant difficulties and to have en-
deavored to meet them. But it seems that Spinoza had no inkling
of such a subjectivistic *cul-de-sac*. More than once the difficulty has
been recognized and slurred over by recourse to the assumed peculiar
fact of the copy-character of ideas of primary qualities as contrasted
with the lack of such imitative representative character in ideas of
secondary qualities. There seems to be no sign of Spinoza's awareness
of such a difficulty and of the availability of the distinction between
kinds of qualities as a mode of outlet from his blind alley. It is an
easy step to pass from Spinoza, the psychophysical parallelist, to the
interpretation of certain passages as standing for a Lockian representative theory of ideas. But the representative function of ideas

in Spinoza is very unlike what that function is generally taken to mean. Ideas for Spinoza represent things somewhat as the equation of a curve stands for the curve, or the law of gravitation for the behavior of falling bodies. The correct understanding of Spinoza's position simply leaves as irrelevant questions the relation of body and soul, of representative idea and thing represented, and allied issues. The vexatious question of the status of the image, for example, is left to one side. These problems, in so far as they exist in Spinoza at all, and in so far as the ordinary formulations of them do not embody a misinterpretation, form a part of the general problem of the relation of the attributes to substance, and arise according to any account whatever of his doctrine. In so far as they depend upon the duality of existence, they are totally irrelevant.

The thesis that is being maintained receives indirect, but substantial, support from a study of Spinoza's statements concerning the attribute of thought and the question of the relation of the attributes of thought and extension to substance. The latter question is the central, and most vexatious, problem of his metaphysics. It will appear in the sequel that the interpretation that has been advanced does not add new complications to the problem; on the other hand, while it does not free the issue of all its perplexities, it at least clarifies it.

We may approach the problem through the attribute of thought. The point involved may be expressed as follows: Do Spinoza's declarations concerning the attribute of thought indicate that he regarded it as a stream of mental and psychical existents, or as the system of logical essences, truths or definitions?

The infinite attribute of thought is "one of the infinite attributes of God, which express God's eternal and infinite essence." [4] Now this attribute is eternal, for every attribute "expresses the reality or being of substance." [5] And every attribute must express the necessity, the eternity, and the infinity of substance. The infinite modes of thought consist of ideas. It follows that these ideas must be eternal. [6] It is this eternity, necessity, and infinity of the attributes that is asserted in the dictum concerning the order and connection of ideas, and gives the idea of substance its rank as the logical, and substance as the causal fountain-head of the infinite mode of thought and extension. "Whatsoever follows from the infinite nature of God, *formaliter*, follows without exception in the same order and connection from the idea of God in God objectively (*objective*)." [7] Shortly after occurs the following illustration: "The nature of a circle is such that if any number of straight lines intersect within it, the rectangles formed by their seg-

[4] *Ethics*, Pt. 2, prop. 1.
[5] *ibid*, Pt. 1, prop. 10, note.
[6] *ibid*, Props. 11, 21.
[7] *ibid*, Pt. 2, prop. 7, corol.

ments will be equal to one another; thus, infinite equal rectangles are contained in a circle.   Yet none of these rectangles can be said to exist, except in so far as the circle exists;  nor can the idea of any of these rectangles be said to exist, except in so far as they are comprehended in the idea of the circle." [8]   There is, then, implicit in the idea of God or substance all the ideas that constitute the modes of thought, as the ideas of the infinity of possible rectangles are comprehended in the idea of the circle.   Furthermore, the idea of the circle is said to be "in God."   Now everything, which *is*, follows necessarily from God; the processions of things and ideas from God are the explication of God's existence and essence through the attributes.   And, finally, we find that "In God there is necessarily the idea not only of his essence, but also of all things which necessarily follow from his essence."   We can not but conclude that these ideas which follow from the idea of God, which form the attribute that expresses the necessity, infinity, and eternity of substance or God, and which are in God, must be eternal, must be truths.   It is impossible to understand how these ideas, occupying such a station and possessing such significations can be identical with a stream of particular psychical or spiritual entities, varying from individual to individual, and having the ephemeral and adventitious character of the individual's experience.   Nor can we arbitrarily select from the totality of putative psychical processes only the so-called "concepts," and hold that Spinoza's words apply to these alone, for emotions, affections, and the rest, have also their ideas and are thereby "represented in the attribute of thought." The stream of the individual's experiences—ideas, memories, illusions, pleasures, pains, sensations, and the like—whether we regard them as psychical or not, can not be equated with the series of ideas which express the essence of God, which are in God, and which follow from the idea of God, "objectively" and "subjectively."

Furthermore, it may be observed, if by ideas Spinoza means psychical states, that is, if the thought attribute be psychical existence, then the ideas are existences.   They must, therefore, possess the particularity and mutability of the concrete events of experience and of physical events or things.   But then they can not be eternal.   For the concrete event or thing as such is not eternal;  it is eternal only in so far as it is an occurrence in the eternal, necessitated system of nature and, as a mode of the extension attribute, in so far forth expresses the essence of substance.   Thus a given motion, say of my pencil, is not eternal, although the concept or idea of motion is.   As essence it is eternal, as event it is not.   But the ideas are said to be eternal.   These ideas, moreover, omitting all question of their imputed psychical nature, are not numerically the equivalents and correlates of the "particular and

[8] *ibid*, prop. 8, note.

mutable" things; they are the truths, the laws, the definitions, the formulae of these things. The concept of a circle is the idea of any circle whatever; the number of possible actual circles is infinite, but their idea-correlate is one. And as a logical entity, it is one and the same for all minds.

If the thought attribute means the organized system of logical essences or definitions, it forms the body of truths, and as such is naturally eternal, necessary, and infinite. The eternity and necessity of the idea mean something quite similar to our meaning when asserting that mathematical principles are eternal truths, or that the laws of science are ultimate. And as a given mathematical principle or scientific law corresponds to or is the explanation of an indefinite number of specific cases or events, so Spinoza's ideas of things are related to things. This account, although it may leave some problems unsolved, at least represents Spinoza as consistent, and spares him the appearance of being oblivious to the obvious difficulties that are occasioned by the rejected construction.

In what light does the problem of the relation of attributes and substance now appear? What solution to that problem is suggested by this interpretation? If the account that has been given is truly representative of Spinoza's doctrine, then an answer to the question based upon this account should promise a closer approximation to the philosopher's solution as he conceived it.

God is defined as a "being absolutely infinite, that is, a substance consisting in infinite attributes, of which each expresses the eternal and infinite essence." [9] The essence of substance necessarily involves existence,[10] or "the existence of substance, just as its essence, is an eternal truth." [11]

The equation, God = Substance = Essence, is the simplest way in which the notion of God can be expressed. For "the existence of God and his essence are one and the same," and "the same attributes of God which explain the eternal essence of God, explain at the same time his eternal existence, that is to say, that itself, which constitutes God's essence, constitutes at the same time his existence." [12] In God, then, essence and existence reciprocally and necessarily involve each other. But with respect to finite things, or modes, this does not obtain, for the "essence of things produced by God does not involve existence." [13] In saying that God is substance, we are saying that he is infinite essence and necessary existence, while modes of thought, or essences, do not necessarily involve existence.

[9] *Ethics*, Pt. i, def. 6.
[10] *ibid*, prop. 7.
[11] *ibid*, prop. 8, note 2.
[12] *ibid*, prop. 20.
[13] *ibid*, prop. 20.

This difficulty now confronts the inquirer: On the one hand, the modes of the attributes are not absolutely the same as God or substance, but are different therefrom in some way; on the other hand, since the attributes express or explicate substance, they must in some sense constitute substance, and be one and the same with it. How is this apparent contradiction to be solved?

The answer seems to be of this nature: God or substance can be understood in two (complementary) ways. *First*, as substance or essence simply, without accidents; this is substance or essence, apprehended *sub quadam specie aeternitatis;* it is substance as the fountainhead, the totality and unity, of all forms or essences, that do or can exist; and as this coherent totality it necessarily exists. Thus we contemplate substance in its infinity, eternity, necessity, potency, and unchangeableness. But, *secondly*, substance can be conceived and apprehended in its explicated form. The attributes represent, express, and constitute substance considered as explicated, unfolded, and displayed. This unfolding is to be conceived, not as an evolution or natural history, but as the logical explication and exhibition of substance. With respect to God as essence, this manifestation is a logical, timeless procession analogous to the explication of the concept of a circle by the deduction of its manifold properties, aspects, and implications. It is the "actual being of the idea." And just as the deductions from the concept of the circle can be regarded as contained within the concept of the circle, so the logical procession of essences can be looked upon as comprised within God as essence. This would be the first point of view, essence without accidents, or essence as unexplicated. With respect to God as essence that necessarily *exists*, that is, *God as existence*, the series of events, or causes, the concrete embodiments of essences in existence, which compose the attribute of extension, is the explication of that existence in actuality. It is *natura naturata*.

The first method of contemplating substance reveals substance as source and dynamic center. The second discloses substance as result and effect. For Spinoza, these are complementary, for substance, or reality, is both at once.

This appears to be the most consistent construction that can be placed upon Spinoza's statements. A similar consistency obviously can not be attained if the thought attribute is taken as a stream of psychical, spiritual, immaterial existents. And reciprocally, the consistency of doctrine put upon this basis strongly suggests the validity of the construction essayed, and the falsifying character of the account based upon what may summarily be called psychophysical parallelism.

And, finally, with regard to the strife between those who uphold the "formalistic" interpretation (taking the attributes as mere modes of intellectual apprehension) and those who maintain the view that the attributes are real properties of substance, the results of this study would favor in the main the second opinion.[14] God possesses an infinite number of attributes, of which thought and extension are two. The system of essences, which forms the thought attribute, is a real property; it is God as thinking being. As comprehended by us, as subjective essences (*essentia objectiva*) contemplated by the understanding, the system of ideas is knowledge of God as thinking and as extended being. Whether our knowledge reaches any further, to any other attributes of God, would seem to be doubtful. The knowledge of God as extended being involves knowledge of existence, of the world of nature. Mind, in a very real sense, is just this system of concepts. The question of whether thought is objectively valid, of how it is possible for understanding to grasp the essences, and similar questions, are foreign to Spinoza's universe of discourse. They are unwarranted intrusions that follow in the wake of misapprehensions and misinterpretations that arise when alien ideas are imagined to be the dominating elements of his doctrine. That understanding is endowed with powers commensurable with the greatness of its appointed task is a conviction that for Spinoza does not stand in need of elaborate justification. For the fruits of reason demonstrate its competency and dominion. The whole of method is but the liberation of understanding and resolute faith in its pronouncements. The province of thought need not be demarcated nor its objective validity proved; for after all, the equation of "to be" with "to be conceived" is the ultimate presupposition of Spinoza's system.

[14] *cf.* Falckenberg, *History of Modern Philosophy*, trans. by Armstrong, p. 127.

# CONCLUSION

The purpose of this essay is to portray the gross misconstructions that have been placed upon the work of Hobbes and Spinoza by taking as the basis of investigation the psychological standpoint of a later day. Such failures to comprehend them as have been touched upon in this paper are derived almost exclusively from ascribing to them the theory of dual existence, which, explicitly or implicitly, has been a characteristic element of latter-day psychological doctrine. The perversions of Hobbes's and Spinoza's meaning are specific instances of a lack of historical perspective and insight—of a tendency to read into beginnings everything that later accrued to a movement. Spinoza and Hobbes, whatever may have been their contributions to the development of our psychology, were not originators of the movement to place it upon the basis of existence as twofold, nor did their teachings impel psychology in that direction. The notion of existence as dual, and of experience as possessing a twofold character corresponding to the two disparate realms of existence with which experience is concerned, is no longer a philosophical abstraction nor a discovery—it is a commonplace of popular speech. With a varying degree of clearness and precision, it characterizes the greater part of ordinary reflection. It is not confined to the lecture-room, but permeates popular thought from street-corner conversation to Sunday-school instruction. "Mind and matter," "soul and body," "the spiritual and the material," and other customarily juxtaposed terms embody this duality of existence as a vaguely grasped truism of discourse. Professor Dewey, in voicing his suspicion of this condition, remarks that "the student of philosophy comes to his philosophical work with a firmly established belief in the existence of two distinct realms of existence, one purely physical and the other purely psychical. The belief is established not as speculative, not as a part of, or incident to, the philosophy he is about to study, but because he has already studied two *sciences*. For every science at once assumes and guarantees the genuineness of its own appropriate subject-matter." [1]

To lay bare the misapprehensions of the meaning of old systems that result from the sway possessed by these notions through their status as almost unquestioned commonplaces serves a threefold purpose. First of all, it leads to a more correct presentation of the history of the systems. And, secondly, it prepares the way for a more adequate

[1] "Psychological Doctrine and Philosophical Teaching," *Journal of Philosophy, Psychology, and Scientific Method*, Vol. XI, p. 505.

account of the origin and growth of the ideas that are responsible for
many of the perplexities that confront the philosopher of the present.
And, finally, it fosters that mistrust of previous speculation which
is a healthy manifestation of the philosophy of the day.

The latter points require some elucidation. In many quarters to-day
an attitude of suspicion, directed not towards the results, but towards
the problems and methods, of previous thought, is a noticeable trait.
We are beginning to doubt the genuineness of the problems which
have been handed down to us. Instead of asking how much truth
and enduring value there is in the historical philosophies, the enquirer
to-day is apt to ask if the problems, or the historical formulations of
problems, which are delivered to us as the supposed foci of investigation, are real and vital. There is a demand for the searching investigation of the presuppositions of old systems and traditional questions
rather than for an evaluation of the old solutions and types of solution.
Instead of taking the attitude that our task is to continue the work of
our predecessors and to solve the difficulties remaining in their systems, we desire to discover whether the problems are legitimate and
inescapable. Those who suffer from such misgivings concerning the
persistent problems of philosophy would prefer to find out what the
problem *is* rather than seek to improve upon the old answers to
problems that may have been radically biassed from the start through
unrecognized presuppositions. The feeling obtains that in accepting
the issues of previous philosophical inquiry, even if we perceive the
inadequacy of opinions on the issues, we may be unwittingly admitting,
as presuppositions, ideas and standpoints that are actually question-
able in themselves; or that, while no longer duped by certain theories
and worn-out dogmas of speculation, we are nevertheless misled by
their after-effects which, although imperceptible, may be influential.

The animus of this attitude may be expressed in this way; if the
historical problem is genuine, human experience at any age will generate it, for it will possess certain traits which reflection feels compelled
to shape into that problem; if, on the contrary, the problems are
artificial, or stated in an unreal form, they are in so far unauthentic,
unreal, and irrational. In the latter case, with changed conditions of
experience, the problem will not be directly generated, but will persist
as a legacy of history. If the problem be unreal, factors alien to the
traits of experience under consideration determined its appearance
and its form. With recognition of the alien character of these factors,
the validity of the problem is impeached. To endeavor to improve
upon the previous solution of such a problem is to perpetuate mis-
directed effort. What is needed is a regenesis of the problem through
an analysis that is at least freed from the pervasive influence of such
foreign elements, and a consequent restatement of the issue in a

form freed from the embarrassments of a mischievous artificiality. In short, the historicity of a problem offers no guarantee of its validity, and a fresh start, a reexamination of the traits of experience, is required.

It does not require much reflection upon the situation resulting from the belief in two distinct realms of existence to notice that it is one calculated to present difficulties. On the whole, it amounts to this, that our deliberations rest upon the dual character of experience and existence as a presupposition, more or less clearly recognized, and when recognized, frequently accepted as valid. "Let a man be persuaded as you please that the relation between psychology and philosophy is lacking in any peculiar intimacy, and yet let him believe that psychology has for its subject-matter a field antithetical to that of the physical science, and his problems are henceforth the problems of adjusting the two opposed subject-matters: the problems of how one such field can know or be truly known by another, of the bearing of the principles of substantiality and causality within and between the two fields. Or let him be persuaded that the antithesis is an unreal one, and yet let his students come to him with beliefs about consciousness and internal observation, the existence of sensations, images, and emotions as states of pure consciousness, the independence of the organs of action in both observation and movement from 'consciousness' (since the organs are physical) and he will be obliged to discuss the type of epistemological and metaphysical problems that inevitably follow from such belief.[2] "The student of philosophy comes to his work having already learned that there is a separate psychic realm; that it is composed of its unique entities; that these are connected and compounded by their own unique principles, thereby building up their own characteristic systematizations; that the psychic entities are by nature in constant flux, transient and transitory, antithetical to abiding spatial things; that they are purely private; that they are open to internal inspection and to that only; that they constitute the whole scope of the 'immediately' given and hence the things that are directly—non-inferentially—'known', and thus supply the sole certainties and the grounds of all other beliefs and knowings; that in spite of their transient and surface character, these psychic entities somehow form the self or ego, which, in turn, is identical with the mind or knower. The summary of the whole matter is that with states of consciousness and with them alone to be and to appear, to appear and to be certain, to be truly known, are equivalents."[3]

One can not refrain from answering affirmatively Professor Dewey's inquiry as to whether these conceptions contain in germ "the substance of the questions most acutely discussed in contemporaneous philoso-

[2] *ibid*, p. 506.
[3] *ibid*, p. 507.

phy." Hesitancy in accepting the questions as genuine and real naturally follows. Unless the duality of existence, which, as a presupposition, activates and directs so much of our thought, is above question, little reliance can be placed upon problems formulated within the limits of that conception. Professor Creighton seems to have had this in mind in the admirable paper in which he considers the question of the possibility of an existential science of psychology.[4]

A study of the origin and growth of these conceptions, and of their influence upon the character of modern philosophy and psychology, should place the epistemological questions of present-day discussion in a clearer light; and if it so happens that these problems are pervaded by a vicious artificiality, the recognition of the fact would facilitate the presentation of the real issue.

The origin of this division of reality into two realms lies, in the first instance, in the Cartesian conception of the dualism of substances.[5] The roots of the doctrine lie, of course, still further back. The notion of immaterial substance becomes clearly defined in scholasticism, and the distinction between matter and form gradually crystallizes into a contrast of spirituality and immateriality to materiality and extension. At the same time, the conception of a plurality of substances, hierarchically arranged from relatively formless matter to form that is pure and free from matter, tends to telescope into a dualism of mind and matter substances. With Descartes the movement is completed.

This, however, is but one of the factors in the genesis of these conceptions. There is another doctrine, characteristic of scholasticism, which converges toward the two-substance doctrine and finally becomes interlaced with it. This is the orthodox epistemological tenet of the cognitive correspondence of idea and thing. The various forms of this theory are at bottom similar in that they look upon the idea as in some sense a copy, a photographic duplication, or imitative representation of the object. To the scholastics, knowledge is the correspondence of forms actualized in intra-organic potentiality and forms actualized in extra-organic matter or potentiality. So long as the notion of a graded hierarchy of substances persists, the correspondence is of one hierarchical arrangement to another hierarchical arrangement. Substances were qualitatively distinct things, ordered serially, beginning with the actual things of the perceptual world, and passing through persons and angels to culminate finally with God or pure form. But through various movements of thought, which

---

[4] "The Standpoint of Psychology," *Philosophical Review*, Vol. 23, No. 2.

[5] The following is a brief statement of the thesis maintained by the writer in an essay originally intended as a dissertation for the doctorate. At the suggestion of Professor Dewey, only those portions of that essay dealing with Hobbes and Spinoza are submitted as a thesis. The theme of the original essay is stated here in order to make clear the general setting of the discussion of Hobbes and Spinoza.

can not be enumerated at this place, the hierarchy is broken up. In the place of a scale of actualities, the several ranks collapse to compose two groups. The process of change consists of two moments. On the one hand, human beings, in so far as they are *thinking* beings (spiritual beings, possessed of a soul), and angels are excluded from the world of nature ("nature" as it appeared to a Galileo), and are no longer regarded as in serial continuity therewith. The assemblage of souls, angels, spiritual forces, and even the Deity, come to form one substantial realm. On the other hand, and coincidently, the world of nature as the assemblage of things loses its qualitative subordination of lower to higher, and in the place of qualitative heterogeneity acquires quantitative homogeneity; it accordingly reduces to one realm of existence. All existents, that is, gravitate toward one of two extremes, while the extremes finally settle down into two spheres not contrasted as contraries, but opposed as contradictories. And in an accordant fashion, with less radical thoroughness, that part of the scale containing minds, angels, and God falls into a substantial continuity approximating the continuity in a quantitative system of nature. The hierarchy of substances is thus concentrated into two substances, and this position comes to be taken over by succeeding speculation in many cases almost without question.

This condensation defines two realms of substantial existence, and coincidently formal, final, and efficient causes become divorced, the formal and final causes being applicable, if at all, only in the world of spiritual substance, while in the world of matter-substance efficient causes alone are operative. Mind and things, knower and known, personality and the world of nature, the soul and the body, idea and thing, fall into such sharp contrast as finally to assume the shape of just so many antitheses. For a long time after the inception of modern philosophy the reciprocal affecting of the two substances was insisted upon or postulated as necessary. Somewhat grudgingly such interaction came to be recognized as a mystery defying explanation, finally to be called by many impossible and inconceivable.

The theory of the cognitive correspondence of species or idea and thing persists alongside of the process of reducing a plurality of substances to two. But the result is the arising of many epistemological perplexities. The situation, in brief outline, is this: knowing goes on in a substantial world, which, by definition, is so unlike the world of the known as to be in sharp opposition thereto, and even antithetical to the assemblage of things known. But knower and known, being in such opposition, the possibility of this cognitive correspondence is itself in question, and yields the first problem of epistemology. The recognition of this situation appears only gradually, as is to be expected. The more keenly, however, the opposition of substances is realized, the more problematic becomes the correspondence of idea to object.

For psychology, the problem is that of the relation of ideas in a realm of spiritual immaterial substance to correspondent things in an extended material substance. With development of the appreciation of the antithesis of the two substances and the parallel growth of doubt concerning the interaction of those substances, the problem becomes acute. A bold science of nature, measuring everything, shoving all qualities into the soul as the easiest method of ridding a quantitative world of them, and intent upon atoms and molecules, sets for psychology a pretty problem. Bidding psychology become "scientific," it offers psychology its instruments of investigation—but at the same time bids it investigate those qualitative phenomena with respect to which this science of nature asserts by implication the unavailability of its instruments. When attention is directed to the physiological process in perception, the relation of thought to things is transmuted into the relation of a mental psychical state to a physiological process in the nervous system which natural science has incorporated into its own world of investigation. The advance of knowledge concerning the world of matter does not abate the exigencies of the situation, but rather accentuates its difficulties. There are two worlds of existents defined by opposition to one another. Psychology in some queer fashion is a science of both, with the task of relating the two assigned it. Psychology must concern itself with both fields, straddling the gap between like a colossus. In short, it has the unwelcome task of relating two spheres that from the outset are declared in effect to be unrelatable. Approaching the spiritual from the side of the physical, with the methods and devices of that field, it runs the danger of falsifying its subject-matter. Approaching the physical from the side of the spiritual, its work seems perverse, unverifiable, and capricious. Rejecting the problem of the ultimate nature of either substance, and in particular that of the soul, as metaphysical and beyond its province, and giving more and more attention to investigations of correspondences of material changes in the sphere of stimuli and nervous processes, to the conscious experience, its subject-matter assumes the form of two series of phenomena, one series physical, material, and physiological, the other psychical, mental, and spiritual. The opposition of two substances is undiminished in the opposition of the two series. With the surrender of the problem of the relation of the two substances, the same problem with respect to the two series must also be surrendered. Psychology, in effect, proceeds on the conception of the parallelism of the series; its problem is the determination of the correspondences; and its postulate, its heuristic principle, only too often taken as an established theory of explanation, is, in narrow

form, psychophysical parallelism. And even the school of interactionists, lineal descendants of those who insisted upon the mystery of
inter-substantial action, do not so much deny the parallelism of the
two existential series, as insist upon their unprovable, but metaphysically and scientifically necessary, reciprocal influence. And the
struggle between parallelists and interactionists leads back again to
conflicting metaphysical systems.

For epistemology, having recourse to this psychology at every stage
of its development, psychological principles aggravate the acerbity
of its problems. For the correspondence theory of knowledge, in its
varying guises, is prejudiced by the psychology to which it appeals,
and for which it is itself largely responsible. The more radically unlike
the series of ideas and the series of events in nature, the more irrational
becomes the assertion of a cognitive correspondence. Yet, be it noted,
just because of this incommensurability of the two series, all that can
be asserted is just some form of this inexplicable correspondence.
Knowing, broken up into a series of ideas, is ruled out of a world of
nature to which that knowing refers, and nature is paradoxically
regarded as known by thoughts that are wholly beyond, and disconnected from, nature. The correspondence being in no wise impeached, it must be taken for granted or asserted as an ineluctable
mystery, or, finally, retained in part and disguised through the device
of ideas of primary qualities. Still more radical measures may be
taken, and the world of the other substance becomes a vanishing point.
We must act as if it existed, but there is no hope of proving it. With
the evanescing of that world, knowledge and the knowing-process
reduces to a concern of the mental world, in truth a "bloodless ballet"
of ideas. The laws of knowing are laws of the combinations of ideas,
discoverable in the series of ideas. But since to be in and of spiritual
substance comes to mean to be in and of the mind; and to be mental
and psychical comes to mean to be in consciousness, knower, knowing, and the known are all literally in consciousness and nowhere else.
To pass from mental substance, from mind, from consciousness, or,
finally, from the ideas of consciousness, to an extra-mental world is,
in terms of the presuppositions, an impossible feat. Like Baron
Münchhausen's feat of lifting himself by tugging at his boot-straps, it
involves a denial of the conditions in which alone the endeavor can
succeed.

Metaphysically, the readiest outlet is a frank and peremptory
repudiation of one or the other substance or of one or the other series.
The history of the two-substance doctrine shows that such an unmiti-
gated dualism will content no one. But the customary fashion of get-
ting rid of it is first to accept it, then to deny it, and, finally, to rein-
troduce it in a disguised form. The assumption is made that one of the

two substances alone exists, although it is defined only by reference to the other and supposedly non-existent substance, and a spiritualistic or materialistic metaphysics results. Or failing so radical an extirpation of one substance, both substances, losing their substantiality, may be conceived as "appearances" or "aspects" of one really real substance. Finally, a still different course may be followed, and one substance be related to the other as appearance to reality, phenomenal being to noumenal. Psychology is put upon these various metaphysical bases, at one time "materialistic," at another concerned with "epiphenomena," or else settling comfortably upon a spiritualistic metaphysics. But in any case, the sciences of physical nature remain and are a persistent challenge to psychology.

The results are many, but all involve in some fashion the after-effects of a metaphysical theory of a dualism of substances. The present dissatisfaction with psychology among psychologists and epistemologists seems to derive its animus from an increasing recognition of this metaphysics that has for so long functioned as a determining presupposition of the science. The notion of the two realms of experience and existence is the point fundamentally involved in the prevailing dissatisfaction with existential psychology in general,[6] and its availability as a propædeutic for epistemology. Professor Dewey, in the article already quoted, points out that "in so far as there are grounds for thinking that the traditional presuppositions of psychology were wished upon it by philosophy when it was yet too immature to defend itself, a philosopher is within his own jurisdiction in submitting them to critical examination."[7] "The prospects for success in such a critical undertaking are increased . . . by the present situation within the science of psychology as that is actually carried on. . . If one went over the full output of the laboratories of the last five years, how much of that output would seem to call, on its own behalf and in its own specific terms, for formulation in the Cartesian-Lockian terms?"[8]

The situation as outlined by Professor Dewey has an important retroactive effect upon the interpretation of the history of philosophy, as the preceding essay has indicated. One outcome of the development of psychology is that so many of the terms of psychology and epistemology, such as sensation, idea, mind, soul, spirit, will, intelligence, consciousness, personality, and the like have acquired connotations that relate them to the spiritual substance side of the duality. The image may be selected as illustrating the fluctuations of terminological meaning, particularly as it is in the early stages of modern psychology so far removed from the psychical. The image has hov-

[6] cf. Creighton, op. cit.
[7] op. cit., p. 508.
[8] ibid.

ered between the two spheres without settling down unequivocally in either realm. Although it rather stubbornly resists being placed in the psychical realm, it has nevertheless acquired a connotation that implies such a status; it is treated in a psychical context. With greater or less clearness, such terms are construed as referring to a psychical principle or its states. As Professor Dewey has asserted, this connotation is not merely sensed by the technical student, but it is almost a dogma of popular usage, and familiarity has engendered implicit credence in the reality of that which the terms connote.

It has been asserted that the theory of a duality of substances, combined with the theory of the cognitive correspondence of idea and thing, were the chief factors in splitting existence into psychical and physical spheres and in developing the doctrine of psychophysical parallelism. But then Hobbes and Spinoza, each of whom insisted upon the oneness of substance, would be expected to afford a crucial test of the truth of the assertion. A study of them should reveal, by contrast, what does not happen when psychological and epistemological investigations are not founded upon a platform of a duality of substance, nor carried on in the interests of such a position. In short, if it is the notion of a spiritual thinking substance that turns idea, concept, and even sensation and perception, into mental, spiritual states of a soul or mind, then investigation might be expected to disclose that in Hobbes and Spinoza there were no "mental psychical states" properly so called. To neither philosopher did the term idea, much less sensation, perception, and image imply an entity in, or a state and manifestation of, an immaterial thinking substance. Historians and commentators have found just such meanings in the work of Hobbes and Spinoza; but their discoveries were possible only because of a preliminary assumption, indubitably to a large extent unrealized, that these meanings were there to be disclosed. We have seen, however, that Hobbes and Spinoza really stand aloof from the movement which leads from the dualism of substances to the doctrine of psychical existence, and the final identification of the psychical, the mental, the conscious, and knowing. It is the unfortunate attitude of assuming their organic involution in this current of development that eventuates in the many artificial perplexities which appear to impede adequate interpretation of their work, and results in a misrepresentation of their qualities of insight and spirit.

## VITA

Albert George Adam Balz was born at Charlottesville, Virginia, January 3, 1887. He attended the University of Virginia, 1905–1912; Columbia University, 1912–1913. Previous degrees: B.A., University of Virginia, 1908; M.A., University of Virginia, 1909. Positions held: Instructor in Philosophy and Psychology, University of Virginia, 1910–1912; University Fellow in Philosophy, Columbia University, 1912–1913; Adjunct Professor of Philosophy, University of Virginia, 1913–1916. Since 1916, Associate Professor of Philosophy, University of Virginia.

Bei Fragen zur Produktsicherheit wenden Sie sich bitte an:
If you have any questions regarding product safety,
please contact:

Walter de Gruyter GmbH
Genthiner Straße 13
10785 Berlin
productsafety@degruyterbrill.com